THE PETOLOGY SERIES

~

LETTERS TO CHARLYE

CAROLINE S. WESTERHOF, Ph.D.

PublishAmerica
Baltimore

First printing

At the specific preference of the author, PublishAmerica allowed this work to remain exactly as the author intended, verbatim, without editorial input.

ISBN: 1-4241-7168-7
PUBLISHED BY PUBLISHAMERICA, LLLP
www.publishamerica.com
Baltimore

Printed in the United States of America

THE PETOLOGY SERIES

~

LETTERS TO CHARLYE

CAROLINE S. WESTERHOF, Ph.D.

Charlye in his chair (every chair was Charlye's!)

THANK YOU TO

GILBERT WESTERHOF,

*Whose greatest gift to me was
The gift of Charlye.*

*It was a sunny day on Long Island, and we were
painting our boat, the "Caroline," and Bert said, "Let's
get a dog," and off we were to the Bide-A-Wee home,
and Charlye was the "friend" we chose, then and forever.*

I thank BERT (GILBERT) and
NANCY WALL
For editing the manuscript.

IT IS THROUGH THE IMPETUS OF
R. GIAN SANTE
THAT THE MANUSCRIPT HAS
BEEN COMPLETED.

IT IS THE WILL OF G-D THAT
CHARLYE
CHOSE US, AND WE CHOSE HIM!

Charlye and Bert

Dedicated to Gilbert Westerhof
whose Intelligence, Love,
Spirituality and Compassion
enveloped Each of Us,
Particularly Charlye,
Who Died in Bert's Arms
February 4, 1988
4:35 A.M.

Charlye, Bert and Caroline
had become a family of three,
and a unit of One.

Charlye was our loving companion,
Sharing in our music, our language,
Our love for each other.

Charlye chewing rawhide stick

I thank my sibling, my brother younger by six years, for his compassion, understanding and caring that has developed through the years since this was first written, whom I very much appreciate today, and I thank my parents for giving me the family I have.

In this the 21st century, my "younger" brother is now looked upon by me as my "older" brother. He, his wife and family, and I are now best friends. Unbeknownst to me until now, my husband, Bert had asked my brother to "watch" over his sister, if he were no longer here. Bert would be proud today, so 1988 was then, and this is now. Thank you, dearest Stuart and Elayne!

PREFACE

Welcome to the Science of PETOLOGY

Animal Souls...Human Souls
by
Caroline S. Westerhof, Ph.D.

PETOLOGY; one of the newest words in our language, and now in print, was created by the author, July 1997. PETOLOGY is defined as the science of animal-human relationships, pet-assisted therapy and the bonding to spirituality and soul, intuition-accessing and meditation combined within both the holistic sense of one's self and of the pet(s).

The father of pet-assisted therapy, Dr. Samuel A. Corson, had specialized in studying the effects of stress and dogs in the 1970's. As Dr. Corson later was to recount it, a severely withdrawn patient in the hospital, a young boy of teenage years, heard the dogs barking and asked to see them. He was allowed to visit the kennel and take one of the dogs for a walk. The teenager, who had barely spoken before to the staff, became so communicative and enthusiastic, that his therapist immediately began using the dog in therapy.

With Mrs. Corson as his laboratory manager, Dr. Corson immersed himself in research in pet-assisted therapy. One of his research projects included a word-by-word analysis that found patients spoke instinctively more often and responded significantly more quickly to questions once dogs were introduced into therapy sessions.

Dr. Corson and his colleagues found that pets were used in psychotherapy as early as the eighteenth century. At least one paper was written on the subject in the 1960's, but Dr. Corson's research is credited with helping to stimulate a surging new interest in the field.

As a result of Dr. Corson's studies and a host of related research by others, dogs and other pets have become commonplace in nursing homes, mental illness and wellness institutions, family settings, and in other environments.

Therapists are discovering that patients in hospices, others who have Alzheimer's and other diseases of dementia, prisoners in correctional institutions, dogs serving persons who are blind or who have multiple sclerosis are some of the environments where the presence of animals has made the environment kinder and more humanly accessible. We are discovering that an animal can be both a source of love and companionship, and a "human" connection where the person may direct his or her own love, care and concern.

Pets, whether for a few minutes or as part of family relations, help to guide us to our higher consciousness of self. This, for me, is the deeper expression beyond our bodies and physical needs. This is the greater world of the nonphysical planes, represented by our souls and spirits. I know that the soul worlds are connected and that all is energy, joined in spirit and soul. Do not ask me how I know...I just know-my body feels "the wind" blowing through it; my intuition tells me, *for I believe, and so I know!*

Pets, particularly, also have a psychic sense of awareness and "speak" the truth! There was the terrier, at the moment her master had died in a local hospital in Germany, who let out a plaintive wail. Her mistress said, "I just know it; my father has just died in the hospital."

There is Missy, whose master has a very quiet wife, who would never respond when he would ask his wife a question. He would look at Missy, and say, "Missy, what do you think?" His wife would lighten up, laugh, and answer to Missy. We have all read the stories of the dog that pulled on his master who was sleeping, because the house was on fire; something was wrong.

Our pets guide us to our deepest self. My mother, in her last weeks, suffering from incurable Hodgkin's disease, would say, when I called her from work, "I am not alone; Charlye is here." My mother would walk down one step at a time, and Charlye would do the same, just one step ahead of her. After each step he would look up to make sure she was okay.

Our pets help us to uncover the unity between ourselves and another. They help us to express the grace of our living, and develop what is already thoroughly human in both ourselves and within themselves—our bonds of love; our attachment and caring.

Many persons feel dissatisfied with a mere ego identity in a functional society. They are in search, and hunger for their deepest self. The essence of spirituality in petology, for both the person and the pet, reflects on the intimacy of their communication experiences through deeper meaning and higher consciousness.

Accessing our intuitive self is part of the process of our mental thinking and higher sense of consciousness. It is both unlimited and a learned phenomena. Through the intuitive accessing of ourselves and our pets we can reach beyond everyday words and experiences to sense moods of people, access other people's temperaments and enhance our decision making ability to sense, feel, hear, taste, see and love. Our pets help us to focus and awaken our best, positive inner channels.

As we evolve in consciousness, it is clear that we cannot do this alone. Through our pets we develop a life affirming

13

expression of our mutual energies in synchronization. Actually, within our inner being, is the pure essence of the life force itself. We try to find out who we are, but find that on this path, if alone, we have much difficulty. Our pets lead us to "go forth into the sunshine," for all is well, if we but allow it in the state of higher consciousness.

Our journey is always a journey back to ourselves. Our pets help to keep us in the present and to stretch beyond self and our own limits. Our pets help us to realize that "at this moment" we are doing the very best that we can.

The concept of our spiritual being as it binds us to our pets includes the following:
- live in the present
- fully engaged in the moment
- ability to love
- ability to care
- ability to experience joy
- ability to be open and awake
- ability to experience humor
- capacity to embrace our own gifts
- capacity to be ourselves and to be loved as we are...

Our pet relationship involves the mirroring back of our very selves. When we embrace our pets, we embrace them as part of ourselves. Our pets give us the courage, the intention, the inner resources, patience, will, energy and compassion to embrace who we and they are, and transform this energy into an aura of light.

At the Monastery of New Skete in eastern New York where the Brothers are training dogs for the encouragement of healthy pet-human relationships, Abbe Xanthias has the belief that "a dog is better than I am, for he has love, and does not judge." The relationships with dogs are far more than what they give. It affects us as human beings. In some ways, says Brother Christopher, "dogs are superior to man; sensorially they are far beyond us...The most interesting portion, however, is on the concept of 'inseeing' or the willingness to really look...and see it as a separate entity in itself, an entity that is truly deserving of a relationship. It is a spiritual approach to life."

So important is the recognition of pet ownership that in May 1998, an insurance company in Ohio, reduced premiums of older customers who have pets. There is enough data to demonstrate that pet ownership reduces blood pressure, lessens risk factors for heart disease, and improves social and psychological functioning. In addition, the pet owner is, for the most part exercising, for they are walking together. It has also been demonstrated that women with dementia who received either pet therapy or exercise intervention had improved irritable behavior after treatment. It is a concrete experience that fills you with a lasting and powerful "persona." Life with a companion animal is a "spiritual practice."

Ralph Waldo Emerson wrote "what lies behind us, and what lies before us are tiny matters compared to what lies within us"...and along side of us to guide us. "...feel your soul at peace, no longer worried or frightened or tense, instead secure in the knowledge of its place here, its reason for being..."(Nancy Wall, "Blessings of the Heart")...and bask in your friend and serenity.

In the last week of April 1998, a nursing home was on fire in the state of Washington. Neighbors and fire fighters rushed in to save the patients and residents. In some instances they were brought to neighbors down the road. As one such neighbor reported, "...we had them touch and play with our dogs, and they relaxed. This reduced the anxiety of the trauma of less than an hour ago."

To the authenticity of the self truth and self wholeness within each of us, it is "you and He..." or *She...*

It's been years
Since there were real Tears

You taught us hugs
Are rich and fulfilling

You taught us paws that touch hands
Frame the spirit of Being

You taught us spirit and soul
Are interconnecting

You taught us color is pageantry
And walks in life are filled with imagery

You taught us we all walk HOME
Hand and Paw
Spirit in Spirit

We are Safe
        As One...

The rain drops will cleanse our souls
The Wind will whisper lessons to learn

We will find truth unveiling
We will meet love and joy

We will meet friends and family
We will have light and hear laughter

We will find true warmth and caring
And through it all...
        We will always be waiting

To hug and to touch
To love and to have

As God holds you
In HIS arms and OURS

As we all walk HOME
Hand and Paw
Spirit in Spirit

We are
Safe as ONE
and
HEALING IN HIS LOVE.

Charlye came into our lives on April 13, 1974. From that day onward our lives changed and our paths converged.

It was Charlye who led the way of where we were to be and why. This is Charlye's story and ours!

This book is dedicated to the authenticity of self and the wholeness and spirit within each of us and our pets.

"Charlye, your Mommy's home."

He came into our home on the afternoon of April 13, 1974, a cool, cloudy, dreary Saturday. According to his papers, Charlye was already about eight weeks old. Little did we know that, for $12.00, we had begun a relationship of enduring love, loyalty, dignity, reality, sensitivity and poetry. No one ever said "there will be limits." No one ever told us "it will end." For fourteen years, almost since the day Bert and I had married, Charlye had been waiting when we came home.

Then, one morning, it all ended.

Charlye's raucous breathing, the chatter that seemed it would break his teeth, ended on Thursday, February 4, 1988 at 4:35 A.M. We, who had always been leaving him, were now left by him...with little notice. I had been lying next to him, stroking him, all night. Yet, even when Bert walked in at 3:15 A.M., Charlye picked up his head to look at him.

Charlye broke our hearts when he died. Somehow, it felt as if the world was going on, but that we had gotten off at the last station.

I was reminded of the week, in 1975, when my mother died. I had said to her "I love you." She responded angrily, "Don't say that." That came back to me at about 3:30 A.M. that morning, as I was about to tell Charlye "I love you." Somehow, remembering my mother's response, I felt stupid.

I had been restless for several nights and was even more so the morning Charlye lay dying. I was jumping out of bed every half hour to see what time it was.

I simply refused to believe I was being a witness to death.

Charlye chose his time to die and it seemed a gift from God. How many people do we know who have died, alone and lonely, separated from the physical and spiritual presence of their loved ones? What gifts of love were bestowed upon the three of us until the very end!

21

Charlye left his home and ours in style: resting on the best mahogany board, cut and polished by Bert, and covered in blankets made by the CB handler, "Charlye's Momma," driven down the hill in Bert's Dutch clean bright red car; then lifted out and cared for by Dr. Jones and his staff who had tended and loved Charlye for the last four and a half years of his life.

March 10, 1988

Charlye had died, yet we had refused to see it coming. As I reflect now; I realize that even his last Saturday, he had walked more slowly and with great effort. I had called to him, "Charlye, hurry, Honey, let's go," and his big brown eyes had looked at me, as always, with love and understanding. Little did I realize that this would be our last Saturday together.

How we miss him! Whenever we leave the house, we return, hoping against hope...maybe we made a mistake; maybe he's hiding under a chair, under a bed. Maybe? But no, the words resound from Bert and echo through the house, "Charlye's gone!" "Charlye's gone!"

Will I ever truly believe that, accept it? Will the tears stop running, the hole in my heart close up? Perhaps, with time.

The week Charlye died, we went through our scrapbooks, pulling out all the pictures of Charlye. We then made a new scrapbook, devoted just to him. We were amazed to discover just how large a part of our daily lives he had become, from our first house in Queens, New York, to the house here, in Prattville, Alabama. What distances we had traveled together...what pain, tears and smiles we had shared during our journey.

Here in Prattville, Charlye had gone into almost every store with me...the tailoring ladies' shop, the printer's, the post office, and the swimming pool store. We made our daily rounds together and went shopping together. When I bought something, no matter what it was, Charlye always had to smell it. "See, Charlye, it's new," I'd say, and he'd put his nose to it and inspect it.

I remember the day I came home with a new pair of red-framed glasses. Charlye looked up at me with those big brown eyes, squinting, staring at this new dimension. To reassure him, I removed the glasses, held them out for his inspection and said "Yes, Charlye, it's your Mommy."

23

Some days, I'd call out, "Charlye, I have a present for you." He'd run to the paper bag and wait, anxiously barking until I pulled out a bag of bones for him. I'd show him the whole package and he couldn't wait until I opened it. He'd sniff each one as I took it out of the bag. When I'd taken about ten out, he'd select three and walk away with the chosen three in his mouth. He was so comical to watch.

He enjoyed such simple pleasures, and it was a joy to us to see him content and happy, pleased with a touch, a lick, a kiss. When Charlye died, I asked Bert to clip a few of his hairs and ever so often I take out the vial we stored them in. To touch those hairs is a reminder that Charlye was, in fact, here and that we were blessed to have had him in our lives.

Someone once said to me "everything has limits." Little did I understand the depth of that statement or the reality it would bring to our lives.

What were the realities of our lives with Charlye? On the day he died, I began assembling a list of how the patterns of our lives had interacted with him on a daily basis.

Each day began with the awakening of Charlye and me. Invariably, I'd have forgotten where I placed my house keys the night before. Charlye would be at my heels and I'd say, "Charlye, I'm looking for my keys. Keys, Charlye." Lo and behold, I'd find them, and when I'd show Charlye, he'd wag his tail and go to the door. We had our own language: it was deep, it was strong…it was love.

I'd put fresh ice cubes in Charlye's water each morning, so our household always had a fresh supply of ice cubes. Now they sit in the freezer until they have to be replaced. The norm of ice cubes was governed by Charlye.

If one has small children, and moves to a new community, the move and subsequent acclimation are made easier by involvement in PTA groups, children's school functions, etc. For us, as two adults, Charlye was the one to help with our assimilation.

I took him to the local shops, where we bought material to make blankets and quilts for him that matched the decor of our new bedroom. When I'd finished making them, on my mother's 1930 sewing machine, I'd say, "Charlye, this is yours," and he'd wag his tail. When I put his new blanket on our bed, he'd jump on it, push it around, and plop down on it with a smile of satisfaction. I'd hug him and get another lick.

We were always doing things together, if I were not working or reading. Charlye was mine and we had a bond. Yet he also needed his space. If I'd been hugging him too long, he'd want to pull away, and usually did. When I'd try to call him back, he'd turn and look and me, but then walk to his chair or bed.

Charlye wanting to be alone

Charlye, too, had set limits. Every chair, every bed was Charlye's. When we bought new leather furniture, we made sure it was low enough for Charlye to be able to jump up on it. At first we covered it with pretty sheets, but he resented that and would push them around until he'd managed to get under them. After about three days of this, we gave in and removed the sheets, which I'm very glad we did. Sometimes, now, when I can't believe Charlye was ever here, I go to those leather chairs and I can see the slight scratches from his nails. I feel reassured and say, "Yes, Yum Yum, you really were here."

Having Charlye sit in my lap was a wonderfully relaxing feeling. His soft, silky hair, his warmth, and his sense of complete trust all came through. Those last few weeks before he died, I had realized what an exhilarating feeling this was, and how nearly impossible it would have been to duplicate. I could have become addicted to holding him, talking to him, loving him. I was unaware of how few "tomorrows" we would have and did not want to believe it could be but a matter of weeks.

I sit before Charlye's lifesize poster, propped on the couch he sat on while I worked in the library or office in the early morning. A flock of birds has flown into the area on its way south. Suddenly, one hit itself against the window pane, fortunately without hurting itself. I was startled to realize it was just about the time I would have been taking Charlye out, and I felt as if it were Charlye saying, "It's O.K., Mommy. I'm here!" The thought brought a smile rather than a tear, and for that I'm grateful.

On the morning of Sunday, January 31st I noticed diarrhea in the library. I immediately called the veterinarian to tell him about it and to tell him that Charlye seemed to have lost weight. On Saturday, I had decided to put him on the scale with me, and discovered he had gone from his usual 33-34 pounds, down to 27 pounds. While that had unnerved me a little, I didn't panic. Dr. Jones said he probably had the flu, to "give him a little chicken and rice," and we made an appointment to see him Monday morning.

As I was cooking the chicken and rice, I showed it to Charlye and told him it was for him, but that he would have to wait until it was done. The expression of joy in his face and the wag of his tail told me he understood. About 45 minutes later, when it was done, I called, "Charlye, your food's ready." I had to add an ice cube to cool it down, though, and he could hardly wait for me to put it in his plate. He jumped up off the floor, and barked so loudly we could hear him through the whole house. I fed him about two tablespoons at a time, at about fifteen minute intervals.

He was thrilled with this new dining fare and I said to Bert, "Maybe Dr. Jones will let me give this to Charlye once a week as a treat." Charlye's last meal...that was our gift to him, a gift he repaid with the joy we experienced while watching him eat and enjoy it. We heard the pleasure and strength in his bark, and realized that he knew we had, once again, done some thing special for him.

We both loved Charlye. Bert would spend each morning having long conversations with him. It was a ritual. Such a ritual that, on Monday, February 1st when we picked Charlye up at the vet's after a day of intravenous feedings, he barked at Bert for several minutes, complaining about all they had done to him during the day. It was Charlye's last conversation with Bert.

28

Bert talking with Charlye

From that time on, all Charlye could do was lie there at look at us with his big brown eyes, pick his head up, and follow Bert's presence. We didn't know if he could still see or not during these last few days. But he knew we were there, and he was still with us, alive.

As recently as December 29th, the veterinarian had given him a clean bill of health. I had come home with Charlye feeling great. He would sit alongside me in the car, pressing his body against me, or sometimes he'd sit in my lap. He seemed to be saying, "If you stop and get out of this car, you have to take me with you." I loved his sense of power and reality, and my feeling that I had to respond to changes in priorities.

I thought back to 1981, when we were living in Virginia Beach. I had joined a health club to do exercises and, if Bert were out of town, Charlye would go with me. I'd park the car, bundle him up in blankets, point out to him exactly where I was going, and run inside. I'd spend my hour exercising, then come back outside and call out, "Charlye, your Mommy's here." His smile, the lifting of his head, made me feel great. Charlye and I had been together, I had given him something new to observe, and now we were going home.

How he loved to ride in the car! Sometimes, he and I would go for a "stationary" ride in the garage at home. I'd say "Charlye, let's go in the car," and we'd both get in. I'd then manipulate the car, while making zooming noises. Charlye'd have his imaginary car ride and I'd laugh hysterically. Bert would see us, and smile at the antics of his wife.

We had a boat in Patchogue, Long Island and Charlye would spend weekends there with us. Often times we'd ship out to Fire Island, to play, to meditate, or maybe to dig clams. Charlye refused to walk on the boardwalk to get to the dog walk, so he was the only dog in the boat community who got carried on his mistress' shoulder. His head held high, we'd parade to this dog offshore landfill. We both felt important, having accomplished our responsibilities for the morning.

Charlye on boat

Until his earthly body was taken away, I had not realized how completely Charlye had enveloped every facet of our lives. We do make promises and set agendas for others with a greater sense of obligation than to ourselves. I knew I needed to get up at a reasonable time each morning because Charlye needed to be walked. Both the beginnings and the endings of my days were governed by my responsibilities to Charlye.

When I began to need some breathing space from the pressures of home and work, I started to walk for about ten minutes on my own each morning. Coincidentally, this began about two weeks before Charlye's death. This walk became something like a light to reach on a hilltop. When I got home, I'd be exhilarated that Charlye would know I was back and be waiting for me at the front door. But when I'd get home, he'd be angry with me. He'd greet me at the front door with a look which seemed to say "Why didn't you take me with you?"

During the last few months, our walks had become strolls, yet I didn't realize Charlye's slowing down was a sign of the path leading toward his earthly death.

I've continued with my morning walks, but since Charlye's death, I no longer leave through the front door, preferring to use the back door instead. I've also started taking a different route, because I choke up when I see the things we enjoyed on our walks together.

To a great extent, the pressures have eased since Charlye's death. Bert no longer feels as competitive, without Charlye and me together. I had never realized, or had forgotten, how closely I could sleep to my husband, because Charlye had always insisted on being in the middle. Both Charlye and I would feel Bert's exasperation.

We miss the hell out of Charlye, but now sleep through the night instead of subconsciously awakening to check on Charlye or to feel him move. As we leave the house, we often turn back and reflect on what a "threesome" we were, how much a part of us Charlye had become, and how much we learned living with him, in life and now in spirit.

I sometimes put nail polish on in bed at night. Charlye always recognized the smell and how he hated it! He'd turn his back on me until the polish had dried and much of the smell was gone. I loved seeing him assert himself each time he saw that polish bottle.

Neither of us was ever alone at night while Charlye was with us, and that was a very secure feeling. In this new age of professional women, I found myself taking frequent business trips. Yet I never felt guilty about leaving Bert because he had Charlye to keep him company. On those occasions when Bert was out of town, I'd lock the bedroom door at night and feel Charlye and I were both safe.

During Charlye's earlier years, when my mother was dying of cancer, I'd call her from work to check on her and she'd say "Don't worry, I'm not alone, Charlye's here." He was an integral part of our family, and he was everywhere. He was Charlye, but he was also part of "us."

When Charlye first came to live with us, my daughter Barri was in her final year of college. I had been carrying Charlye up and down the stairs until finally, in those first few months, he stood at the top of the stairs and cried. About that time, Barri came along. She sat on the steps, sliding down one at a time with Charlye, as he went down. She did that up and down the stairs, as he went with her, and within fifteen minutes he was walking the stairs. I was the one who had said, "Do it, take the plunge," but Barri had provided the example. She later trained to become a psychologist.

Charlye always waited for us to come home from work, usually in the living room. If Bert and I came home separately, which we sometimes did, Charlye would rush past whichever one of us had come in, to look for the other.

When we came home, we always gave him a piece of his food as a treat. But never, not even during his last week of life, would he take it until he had kissed us "Hello!" It was an exquisite feeling, but only today do I understand the depth of his love. Yet, as much as I loved Charlye, I think I took him for granted.

When I'd awaken in the morning, I'd think Charlye was still asleep, and go out to work in the library or office. Within half an hour, he'd find me. It was fun to watch him looking for me. I'd say "Hi, Charlye," and give him a hug and a kiss. Then I'd open the door and let him out. He'd never go out alone. When he came back in, he'd join me in the library, jump up on the couch and settle in to watch me work. He always seemed to know when I was working.

When I'd bring Bert breakfast in bed, Charlye would jump or I would lift him, onto the bed. The last piece of Bert's Dutch rusk, a hand-toasted cracker, was Charlye's, and he always demanded his share. Many times, while Bert was having breakfast, I'd say "Charlye, let's go out for your walk," only to

Barri snuggling with Charlye in Charlye's bed

have him ignore me. He wouldn't leave Bert, for fear he'd lose his bite of cracker. Then Bert would say "Go with Carol. I'll save it for you." Out we'd go, he'd do his business, and we'd rush right back in.

When Bert started eating Dutch almond cookies, Charlye demanded his share of those, too. When he died, I thought I'd never be able to eat those cookies again without choking. It was at least three weeks before my emotions calmed enough to allow me to peacefully take a bite.

Charlye even became a component of my American Government lectures, and sometimes accompanied me to Hostos Community College when it was in the South Bronx. Our house in Queens had a mail slot in the door, and one day Charlye tore up a letter the mailman had dropped through the slot. What remained of the letter talked about a meeting scheduled for "Tuesday." However, because Charlye had destroyed the section of the letter which gave the date of the meeting, it was impossible to determine which Tuesday. This became an important part of my American Government lectures, stressing the necessity of "receiving complete information," as well as the importance of getting the whole picture.

I had also used him as an example of "pressure politics." Charlye would ask for another cookie, and I'd say "No, you've had enough." He'd begin to bark again, and continue to do so every few seconds. If that failed, he'd then raise his front leg and press it against my thigh in a further plea. By continuing these antics, Charlye usually got his extra cookie. I've always loved this concept of pressure politics: if you want, you must ask; if you feel you should have, you need not accept "no." And, much like the deaf students of Galaudet College, who demanded the removal of the College President, "You do not let up." You must know what you want in a positive vein and go after it. Charlye was a beautiful example of the development and use, to its fullest extent, of pressure politics: how to get from there to here. Had he walked away, he would not have gotten that extra cookie.

It has always given me a sense of romance to drive down the hill in old, quaint Prattville, go to the newspaper machine and buy the daily New York Times. I'd put my quarters in the machine and here, in of all places, next to the old, historic post office, I'd pick up a New York Times. Many times Charlye accompanied me on that errand, and since his death I no longer buy that, or any other newspaper. Any sense of romance has vanished. During this time I've tried to comprehend my feelings and the only rationale I've been able to arrive at is a sense that somehow I'm trying to stop the clock, to hold back the calendar. Perhaps February 4th can be prevented from ever occurring, and we won't have to lose him. Combined with this is my disbelief that Charlye could have died so quickly.

Yet did it all come about that suddenly? When I think back, I realize Charlye's appetite had been off since early January. We had even talked with the vet about it. We had thrown away what was left in one bag of food, thinking it might have picked up some odors from the closet. When we opened the new bag, though, Charlye would take only a couple bites and then stop.

I know I could not have changed Charlye's history or the pattern of his life, but perhaps, had I understood he was dying, I'd have been more gentle with him, loved him more, spent more time at home. I would have…what would I have done? Would anything have been done differently? Would the outcome have been any different? I'll not know until I meet Charlye again and we can talk about it.

In the weeks immediately preceding Charlye's death, Bert had been growing increasingly upset. He just didn't feel well, and had been taking his pressures out on Charlye and me. Though Bert didn't realize why at the time, Charlye had been trying to push closer to him in bed at night, which wasn't helping matters. Two weeks before he died, Charlye had been sleeping with me. He'd be on the bed, but didn't seem to feel the need to press close to me. We were just together. That last week before Charlye died, Bert had said we could put him alongside us in the bed. I propped up his pillows, nearly to the level of the bed, and put our blankets over him. At first he seemed unhappy, but then settled down. I touched him under the covers all night. The thought that perhaps I mentally hurt Charlye during these last weeks of his life really upsets me.

His last Saturday here, I came home for a half hour between meetings. He walked very slowly and when I left he didn't come back to the kitchen to see me off. I thought he might be tired, so I went back to the bedroom and said "Charlye, I'm going." When I returned a few hours later, I gratefully realized Brad (his dog sitter) had been here and had taken Charlye out while I was gone.

I never thought Charlye would slip away from us, but that's the way it seemed to happen. Could I...would I have held him tighter if I had known? Though I'm grateful Charlye died in our bed, amidst clean sheets, with us holding him, it still hurts to realize how quickly he was gone. I realize that for him to be with us through his last moment was a gift from God. We knelt and said our prayers. How it hurts to know he slipped away, without my having hugged him more. I'd been afraid I'd upset him during the night and morning of his dying, so had just touched him. But, oh, how it hurts.

Camera America has redone Charlye's poster and his coloring is magnificent. In this more natural coloring he looks happier. Yet I can't bear to discard the other one, or to "hang" him on the wall, so his poster rests on the couch where he always sat. I'm surrounded by his photographs, and the early morning hours I would have spent with him I now spend writing about him and learning to meditate and channel. It is comforting.

Yesterday brought a painful realization and yet, at the same time, a cleansing, for which I'm grateful. For two days I'd been sobbing uncontrollably, and I'd been asking God to please remove my lower energies and replace them with my higher energies. About an hour later, this realization came to me boldly and clearly:

Charlye, dear Charlye, how much you have taught me and how much your person has held my love, my anxieties, my poetry and rhythm for living. I had been fastening all my love on you; you had been compensating for the warmth and true love I had been yearning for, yet not receiving from Barri, as a daughter and from Stuart, as a brother.

I had been masking, making believe that their true love was there. When you died, the make-believe I had created for

Barri and Stuart suddenly unfolded...nothing remained but empty balloons of emotions. Each is busy in his or her own world, and the warmth and concern which would have enveloped me for another was not there for me from them.

It suddenly hit me yesterday, Charlye, that you had been the focus of my motherly and sisterly warmth and love. I had not wanted to see or believe that Stuart or Barri could not recognize our emotional hunger for family, or, even worse, that they just couldn't be bothered with Bert and me. We were O. K. to receive gifts from them. They can mail us a card here and there, or call a florist to have flowers delivered. But the real strength of their warmth and love had never been there...I had been pretending it was.

Thank you, dearest Charlye, for showing me the realities of love and caring. Dearest Charlye, I will try to stop crying, but, oh, how you're missed!

Who would have thought, Yum-Yum, that the couch you always sat on would now have your lifesize portrait on it, or that I'd be sitting here, looking at it, writing to and about you? I don't see your beds in their places anymore, unless I focus on them; I don't see your food dishes or the food canister. I just miss you, Yum Yum, your presence and the pleasure of doing things for and with you.

I remember when I let you out the patio door one morning that last week. You looked at the steps, hesitated, then slowly went down. I remember thinking maybe the steps were too much for you, but you made no complaint so I just let it pass.

I noticed you were spending more time in your bed, but I thought "that's O.K.," because at night you'd have gotten into bed with us. The treat of each passing day was that, at night, you'd be sleeping with us. You always wanted to get under the covers, but I knew you couldn't breathe as well under them anymore. I'd then try to make believe and cover you with just the sheet, leaving your nose peeking out. Sometimes you let me, other times you didn't. Either way, it was funny.

If you had a problem or you didn't feel well, you'd always jump off the bed. You didn't want to vomit or have an accident on the bed. Even when you had surgery on your back legs, you held your urine rather than wet in the bed.

When you first died, Charlye, I couldn't believe it. Since then, I've calmed down some and begun to realize that you had been a part of our lives and that I had no business denying the gift of you to myself.

Yesterday was the first day of Spring, Charlye, but you weren't here to enjoy it. How you loved to "smell the wind." You'd go outside, lift your face up, and with your neck stretched you'd look as if you were smelling the wind. I sometimes do that now and as I picture you in that stance, I walk taller and straighter. I, too, am "smelling the wind," Charlye, just as you taught me to do. But it hurts that you're not here to smell this newest Spring with me. Like someone smelling ammonia salts for revival; that's how joyfully I'd watch you smelling the wind.

Cele Hirsch's sister died March 9th. When I spoke with Cele this week, she said, "We didn't know how sick she was." Yet, her sister had had cancer for the last few years. Dearest Charlye, don't we all say that when someone we love dies. I didn't know how sick you were, either.

I kept calling Dr. Jones, and even ran down the hill with a sample of your stool, which was a reddish-orange color. Dr. Jones had said, "I know what it is. It's nothing!" I didn't ask, "Oh, what is it, then?" Instead, I simply went back up the hill, grateful he had said it was nothing.

Perhaps we always say, "I didn't know how sick he or she was," when, in reality, we just can't let ourselves admit or accept how sick a loved one was. Our hearts wouldn't let us know and yet there's a subconscious feeling that God knows what has to be. The week we were told you were very sick, Bert prayed for a miracle. I felt stupid praying for a miracle. Intellectually, I knew you were dying, but could never believe it or accept it. Any other time you had been sick I had prayed and prayed that you would get well. This time, I just prayed, dearest Charlye, perhaps already knowing, at some level, what the outcome was meant to be.

When we were scheduled to attend the March business convention, I couldn't make plans ahead of time. After your death, I couldn't make myself make the plans. I didn't want to leave you. Those last few weeks, I'd had an extra chair in the living room, so I could sit right next to you and touch you. Despite Bert's objections to the extra chair, I refused to move it. I knew how you loved to be touched and wanted to be where I could sit next to you. I can't bear to hang your pictures on the wall, away from us. Nor can I bear to leave a picture of you at work, because you didn't like to be left there. I want to be enveloped by you on the couches where you sat, next to the chairs you sat on.

March 23, 1988

Demise   Guilt   Anger   Resignation   Acceptance

Dearest Charlye, I keep confusing today with Thursday, but it's not. Tomorrow it will be six weeks since I've touched you or hugged you, yet you've not been far from us, Yum Yum. You've been in our thoughts and minds. Nearly every morning I sit on the couch in the library looking at your life-size photograph, resting on the other couch. It makes me feel good to see you there, to talk to you. If only I could transform its dimensions and you could talk out! Sometimes my inner thoughts are so strong, I go and touch the few hairs Bert clipped from you the day you died.

What you have wrought for us in learning and loving! The other day our freezer of twenty-one years finally gave out. We threw away much spoiled food, including the chicken I had bought in hopes the vet would say I could give you a little bit once a week as a treat.

I then asked Bert to help me clean out the refrigerator in the kitchen. Lo and behold, you must have been watching, for I found one piece of your food. What a gift! I put it with a couple of the dog bones I'm saving.

Your death has taught me there are limits in life. I had thought I could hold back your death; that surrounding you with Mother's bed jacket and blanket would infinitely protect you and that you would live on in body forever. I now wear the bed jacket, dear Charlye, and have sewn the edges with lace, some fifty years old, that my father had.

Your death has taught me everything has an end, dear Charlye, so I'm starting to throw out or give away much around the house. You have awakened me, dear Charlye, in life, in death, and in spirit. There is so much I have learned, and each day there is another awakening.

Several weeks before you died I'd seen a rubber band lying outside the kitchen door. It was still there the day we carried

44

you outside to the red Cadillac to your final resting place. It was there when we came back after running away for some ten days. It was still there last week. I've just looked again, Charlye, and it seems to be gone, either picked up by someone or taken by the wind.

That circular rubber band was a linkage for me, dear Charlye. In its unbroken dimension in seemed to me to connect the past with the present with the future. In its total self, it had moved from one spot to another, yet its circular, physical property had not been broken. Your death has not broken your relationship to us. Rather, it's become a connecting part of our relationship, perhaps reaching more deeply. Though I can no longer touch you, I have gone more deeply into our spiritual relationship and am learning so much more about your meaning, to us and to all of life. You are quite a teacher, dearest Charlye, in life and in death.

Saturday

There's one picture of you I took on December 20th. From it your eyes follow me wherever I go, just as they did when you were here. Please, dearest Charlye, go with me all over. I love it. I'll learn that I don't have to see your earthly body in order to touch you and love you. I can do it in my mind.

I forgot to tell you, but you probably already know: Bert picked up that rubber band and used it in the "swimming pool general." So, even in its philosophical relationship to us, lying on the ground, it became functional and utilitarian, which has always been a part of our natural realities.

Today is the six-week anniversary of the day you left us, dear Charlye. Here on the couch where we laid you out in style, I sit looking at your magnificent photograph. I guess I've never thought much of beautiful family portraits, which others have taken. I wanted to be the one to take the pictures, and to cherish the memories of that, which I myself had taken. Is that why we have no family portrait of the three of us, dearest Charlye? Someone else would have had to take it.

You were lying on the living room floor. I opened the patio door so you could look out, thinking maybe tomorrow you wouldn't be able to see the fresh outdoors you so loved. Yet, I couldn't say you were dying, Yum Yum. Dr. Jones hadn't yet told me you were terminal, just that you were very sick. How I functioned, dearest Charlye, rather than just hugging and loving you.

We're cleaning and reorganizing parts of the house and it seems so strange. Last night Harold Mims and his wife came over to put new floor-to-ceiling wardrobe cabinets in the back room where the exercise equipment is. After serving refreshments and dinner, dear Charlye, I had to wipe up the crumbs that had fallen on the floor. No more Charlye to clean them up for me.

We stay later at work these days, and then have dinner out. There's no more running home to walk you or talk to you. I miss you very much, Charlye, but I am learning to accept that fact, that I can't touch you or hug you, or laugh and smile with you in body. I'll always talk to you, though, and feel you're with me, just as I always did when we were miles apart. Even when we were in Africa, Bert and I would look at our watches and say, "Well, Charlye's been walked or such." I used to wonder if you knew we were thinking about you.

You sometimes had it hard, too, Charlye. I know you didn't understand when we had to move from Virginia Beach. You walked around the house in circles for three days. I'd pick you up, hug you, and "Charlie, it's okay," but it wasn't enough comfort for you. The day we left Virginia Beach, you were the first one in the car. You jumped in like a jumping jack, and sat either next to me or on my lap all the way to Alabama. We didn't know you were sick then, either.

Charlye at the beach on Fire Island in New York State

The day after we arrived in Prattville, you and I stopped at the Animal Medical Clinic and met Dr. Jones. After tests, they diagnosed your pancreatis and told us there was a fifty percent chance you'd make it. That was June 29, 1983, and make it you did, Yum Yum! We took you up and down the hill twice a day for intravenous feedings. You soon began feeling better and pulling the needle out of your leg. Within ten days you were back in shape and, in fact, Dr. Jones said you were ten pounds over weight. One of our most painful experiences together was trying to adjust your diet to help you maintain your best weight. I felt mean and angry at myself, that I couldn't give you what you wanted.

I also had to eliminate your cookies. Can you imagine me having to convince you that a nugget of your regular food was now going to be a "treat?" What subterfuge! We got over that one too and, if I remember correctly, it didn't take long, either, Charlye. Within a couple of months we had both relearned our patterns of behavior. I was none the worse for it, and you were better.

We used to walk a lot through downtown Prattville and what a romantic, and sometimes, a historically painful experience for me. At 6:00 A.M., Charlye and Carol walking through historic Prattville, an old Southern Confederate town; past the old factory, the Jefferson Davis statue, the torn up streets, the worn out stores filled with stories and history, past the rings used to hold slaves for sale, past the creek. This was history "in the raw." Coming from New York City, and being active in the intimate diversity of the city—firends, relatives—a mixture of ethnicity—race, religion—witnessing this historical reality was always painful.

Together we discovered things and people in downtown Prattville; Mr. Oates at Progress Printing, Mr. Scott of the Post Office, Margaret McGhee, George Walthall, and the strikers at Continental Eagle. One morning we met a man from New York, and how excited I was! His car had New York plates and was filled with all kinds of cloth and fabric. When I asked him what he was doing there, he said he was a fabric dye salesman and that he made periodic visits to the local factory.

Daniel Pratt had come from New Hampshire in the 1800's to start the first cotton gin factory here, then a fabric factory sprang up next door, along the river. Now, in the 20th century, a transplanted New Yorker was meeting another New Yorker along the creek banks in Prattville. And you, dearest Charlye, were all a part of that!

People would stop and talk to us because you were with me. Everyone said you were so pretty and I would pipe up, "Sweet and delicious, too!" Sometimes you'd stand there looking around while I chatted. Other times you'd start barking, "Let's go!" It was delicious and invigorating, dearest Charlye, to have you rule our walk.

Everyone knows that it was you who found this nice house we're living in. We were walking up the hill and discovered this interesting, modern-looking new home. As it was unoccupied, we walked around it and found the back door open. I knew immediately it was a good house for you. The windows were low, almost to the floor, so you'd be able to look out. It was bright and cheery and, for us, had a good-size family room which could be used as a library.

Since your earthly body has left this house, I'm recognizing that everything in life has limits. I'm beginning to put the house in order; books and papers which I'm sure I'll not be needing for research, re being discarded, clothes not worn are being given away. Things are being put into such order, dear Charlye. What, I wonder will the orderliness feel like? Will it destroy my personality? Will I be less creative? It is an interesting feeling to watch all this happening. Deep down, I am pleased, dearest Charlye, and once again it is you who has led the way.

Last night I slept in the guest room, your last resting place here. I thought it would be painful, but I slept through the night and felt good about it. I'm beginning to accept you as my spiritual guide, Charlye, and that fills me with a sense of beauty, comfort and protection.

Now that there aren't too many of your hairs around, I sure miss them. I can wear navy slacks or the navy jacket without having Bert tell me to "Brush the dog hairs off." It never occurred to me that there would come a day when there would be no more dog hairs. When I find them now, I treasure them. I also feel they're a sign that your spiritual presence is here. There are still a few on the purple blanket, and unless it gets badly soiled, that blanket will never be washed.

You loved the burst of Spring and the smell of wind and it saddens me that you're not here to experience it with me. Then again, dear Charlye, perhaps you're experiencing new bursts of energy and sunlight in your metaphysical state.

Dr. Jones kept you together. You came back beautifully from your two pancreatic attacks, recuperated from the operation on your back legs, survived having your teeth cleaned and suffered a minimum of fleas. You enjoyed the wind on the back deck, running errands with me, traveling in the car, and just being together. Even though you've died, your urn is here with us in Prattville, and will stay with us wherever we may wind up.

On Friday it was pouring outside. On those days, a small part of me finds comfort in not having to "walk in the rain," or having to drive downtown to a covered shopping mall. I'm also grateful we had you cremated rather than buried. It would break my heart to think you were in the cold, water-soaked ground, with the storm and its rain pounding on your grave.

Having your urn gives me peace, and more of a sense of your earthly self, though metaphysically I shall always feel your presence and know you're near. I'm glad you weren't cremated until the day after you died; it lets me feel you had a day for your spirits to leave your earthly self.

Friday night I made oatmeal for us for supper. In a flash, dear Charlye, I was ready to put my plate on the floor for you. As I was eating my oatmeal, I thought, "Gee, this is nice and smooth for Charlye." In less than that split second, I realized your earthly self wasn't here. Bert felt the same way.

I've learned, dear Charlye, that many of our behaviors are learned responses. We may build these responses on love or need, but we have taught them to ourselves. In a sense, we have taught each other that, "Charlye can lick this last drop of oatmeal." Now that your earthly self is not here, we'll have to learn another response. Knowing these actions are learned responses helps the grieving process. Before I understood this I thought all of our actions toward you were out of pure love. Now, however, I can learn to separate this feeling and emotion of love from the learned responses. When the learned responses are unlearned, the pain is not as great.

Whether getting the mail, or the newspaper, or just putting the garbage out, these were all things we shared. Learning to do them without you were so painful, but now we share our love and that's a greater feeling of peace than thinking about the routine I had established; putting your fresh food and water down, placing your food in the same spot near the stove, making sure we always had fresh ice cubes. Realizing there was no longer any need for fresh ice cubes resulted in a tearful few moments. Where your canister of food stood on the stove, there is now a plant. I do keep the glass of the Yarzheit candle, which I lit the day you died, on the stove. It helps me to separate your earthly body from your spiritual one, and I need that.

We had always looked forward to the weekends because they gave us more time to spend together, and I loved it. We didn't have to rush out of the house, we could relax at home, go for a ride, or just putter around. The weekends made a difference for us.

Now, though, the weekends bring us heavy hearts. When we come home, there's much to do, but no Charlye with whom to laugh and smile and share. We miss you, Charlye, so much.

I touch your urn and picture each day for a split second, and hope you feel it. Do you? I do this in recognition of how close you always wanted to be to us, and usually manage to smile, rather than cry. I just say, "Hi, Charlye," or "Hi, Yum Yum." I somehow sense that you feel it and I feel we're walking and doing things together. It makes me feel better.

We attended a Budget Convention in San Diego March 3-10th, dear Charlye. It was almost to the four-week anniversary of the day your earthly body left us. It was an interesting trip in that, without asking, I found your presence around me and it was as if on this trip you could come with us.

It was also interesting because before you died, I kept wondering about this convention, but couldn't make the plans or reservations to handle it. I didn't even want to talk to Elliott about staying with you. I just couldn't think about leaving you, but I didn't understand why. Was I feeling something, dear Charlye? Was I afraid to feel something?

I still come home at night thinking maybe it'll all go away, maybe it's all a mistake, maybe you'll step our of one your pictures. Dear Charlye, I wish I had the guts to join you...to make it easier for all of us.

Days like this past Sunday, when we're home most of the day, are difficult. Knowing you're not here in your earthly self leaves a heavy ache which hurts terribly. You're missed so much.

We made the poster-size photo of you to hang in the new office. I don't know if I'll be able to do it, though, as I know you didn't like to be left alone at work. I don't know what I'll do, Charlye. Please help me make that decision.

The newspaper shop at the hotel had two plush, life-size dogs for sale. One was a beagle and looked almost like you. Each time I looked at it I felt a different sense of how you were communicating with me. The first time I looked at it, I almost hadn't seen it. Then I turned around and felt a big smile on my face and on your's. I felt good. You had, indeed, come through the walls and flown the sky, in your spiritual self.

The next day, I went back to purchase some earrings and didn't look at "you." I turned and felt you were looking at me sideways, with your head tilted as you sometimes did. It seemed you were saying, "You know, you shouldn't buy those earrings." I smiled and felt good that you were chastising me. It was just what you would have done when I didn't do what you wanted.

Another sign I've received from you came when we were eating at the Sandwich Shop Restaurant in one of the San Diego malls. Here we were in March and yet their register tape read February 4th...they hadn't yet changed the date. I smiled and through my tears felt good to know you were with us. So, although I have no pictures of you after February 4th, I now have a register tape. Funny, isn't it, Yum Yum! It was a comforting feeling.

In San Diego, I was still suffering the pains of grief and couldn't put your death in a perspective of calm reality. Finally, on March 9th, I awoke and said, "I promise I'll not cry; I promise I'll look at a picture; I promise I'll not mention your name." I finally visualized your death as a very deep wound inside of me. If there's a wound, one does not take the bandage off until it has healed; otherwise, you'll pull the scab off and the blood will ooze again. I felt if I could look at my grief like that wound, covered with a bandage, I could control better my ache and pain. In my functional way, it helped somewhat, dearest Charlye. Now I try to smile whenever I see you or think about you. It doesn't always work.

Last night I was redoing my closet, discarding clothes no longer worn. How I smiled whenever I touched clothes, which still had your hair on them. I find, though, that I have another small problem, dearest Charlye...I can no longer distinguish between your hair and mine! It's a rather delicious situation.

So many thoughts go through my head, dearest Charlye. I haven't put an alarm clock on the night table next to my bed since your death. It's been eight weeks today, Charlye, and it hurts. I selfishly miss hugging you, touching you, talking to you. Bert says he sees you sometimes, wagging your tail and smiling at him. I need to be surrounded by your pictures to see your presence, particularly that photo from which your eyes follow me.

I don't worry now, when I go out of town, about what you're doing "at that moment," or wondering if Brad walked you yet or is Mrs. Byrd there now, so you're not alone. When we'd go away, I wouldn't change my clock. I'd keep it on the time where you were, so I could identify what you were doing at any given moment.

When it rains I no longer worry about you not liking the rain. Instead, I think, "maybe it's better that Charlye's not here." Does it rain where you are, Yum Yum, or does the sun always shine? Remember we sometimes went to the Winn Dixie shopping mall and I'd walk you under the marquis? Sometimes, if I was too tired to make that trip, we'd walk with an umbrella and I'd hold it over you rather than me. Then we'd come in and I'd dry you off.

Well, we're really into Spring now, dear Charlye. Is it always Spring where you are? I dropped some crumbs from Bert's Dutch cookies on the floor this morning, and was ready to leave them there for you. Before I could call, "Here Charlye, see," I remembered you're not here. I also realized that in your own small way, you helped me keep the house clean.

It's April 1st, Charlye, eight weeks and one day since we last hugged and touched you. The flowers are coming into bloom. This morning, one particular bush was swaying in the wind. Two different birds flew to our bedroom window within seconds of each other and literally peered in. Both Bert and I felt it was your way of telling us you're with us. In fact, Bert told the first bird, the elder of the two, "Tell Charlye, Hello."

Have you met Dee Dee Stier, Charlye? He's Zodie and Bul's son. Zodie asked me this morning how I've been doing and I told her I'd been sobbing terribly for you on Tuesday night. She told me I'll feel the pain of missing you more acutely when I'm tired.

The last time she and I visited, she showed me the notebooks her son had written during his illness. She also tells a story about a visit Dee Dee had from a priest, during his illness. Dee Dee asked the priest, "Do pets have souls and spirits?" The priest said, "No."

"In that case," said Dee Dee, "I don't need to hear what you have to say. I know pets have souls and spirits." I love that story, dearest Charlye. It makes me smile. We know there's a spiritual world, Charlye, and that you and Dee Dee are helping us feel your presence and to smile rather than cry.

I feel very strongly that you are our higher spirit. You're a linkage to a greater world and environment. Mrs. Talley said you're in a happier place, and I know that, but selfishly I miss you terribly.

Isn't that terrible, Charlye? There's no fun anymore in "stealing" napkins from Wendy's to wipe you with when you've been out. For Christmas in 1986, you were even promoted to Merry Christmas napkins. I doubt there was any other dog in the country that was wiped with Wendy's Merry Christmas napkins. Now they have no purpose other than what was intended, yet serve as a reminder of you.

These memories bring laughter and joy to us, dear Charlye. They help us feel your presence, and reassure us of the reality of your being and self.

I didn't write yesterday, Charlye. It was the Sabbath and the first day of Passover. I wanted to put a piece of matzoh in front of your picture, but then thought that was probably silly. You know if you'd been here, I'd have given you a sliver and hoped Dr. Jones wouldn't be angry with me.

We spent the entire day at home, and from time to time, we felt that ache in our hearts, like a hole that doesn't close, because you weren't here. I felt your presence very strongly, particularly on Friday, dearest Charlye. My body felt lighter, like a lilt in the air. When I did my exercises, that one plant outside the exercise room window was moving; it was the two birds which had peered in the bedroom window for a few seconds. They make us both feel as if you're close at hand. I dozed off in the early evening and awoke with a start, feeling you were really close. When I realized you weren't here, I felt somewhat angry.

Yesterday, Bert and I were reading, catching up with all of our newspapers, some of which were dated before you died. I guess that hurt, too, trying to pull those days back, but I found many linkages. Have you seen our parents yet? Or Uncle Sam? Or Dee Dee Stier? We found some beautiful advertisements for Puerto Rico and I thought of my father. There was reference to a poem Grace Kelly had written about a rose, how special it was, and that it was much more than a flower. That caused me to think of my mother. We read about the Vliegele Hallander, the flying Dutchman, and the Netherlands, and I thought about Moeder, Bert's Moeder.

Then I said to Bert, "You've got to find something about Charlye." He was reading about drug raids in Miami and saw a photo of a beagle wearing a coat with "U.S. Narcotic" on it. The dog was standing on two legs, sniffing in a barrel, and I said to Bert, "All our family is together for the holidays, and they're giving us signals to let us know." How we love you, dearest Charlye, and how you've strengthened us in life and death.

Charlye in winter coat

Friday morning, Bert left a plastic bag on the bed, after removing if from his freshly cleaned clothes. I said, "You can't do that, Charlye'll get into it." He laughed and said, "You wish! " I joked back, "Not really, if Charlye were here you wouldn't have left it."

I hope the day will come when I can smile, without choking up about all of you, Yum Yum!

April 8, 1988

It's now Friday, Charlye, and I haven't written since Sunday. Monday we were rushing around getting ready for our trip to Detroit. We left the house about 6:00 A.M. Tuesday and arrived in Detroit that night. We left about noon on Wednesday, stayed at the Radison Inn, in Cincinnati (where you would have been permitted to stay) and arrived back in Prattville about 11:00 P.M. Thursday night. So many things to tell you, Charlye, though you were with us all the way, so you may know even more than I do.

I sit on the couch in the library looking at your poster picture. It is comforting to see you life-size in your familiar position on the couch.

When we left here Tuesday morning, there was some sense of pain. I didn't have to wake up in a hurry to walk you. I didn't have to make sure the refrigerator was stocked for your live-in sitter/companion. I didn't turn around as I walked out and say, "Dear God, please take care of Charlye and let me see him when I get back." No, dear Charlye, this time you were going with us, and yet I was crying because I couldn't touch or hug you.

Whenever we'd left before, I'd felt sick to my stomach. I'd tell you we were going, tell you who was going to take care of you, then ask you if that was O.K. Each time, you'd wave your tail back to me, as if you were saying, "Go. It's O.K.," and I'd feel a little less guilty. This time there was none of that; just tears, a feeling of quietness, and an ache in my heart.

Bert and I talked a lot about you on the trip up. We had also brought our tapes for the car tape player. We usually forget to take them, but this time Bert remembered. After we'd played a couple, I went through the box looking for some more. I pulled out "Reggae Speaks," something I'd obviously taped from somewhere. The date on it was July, 1982, which was when we were still in Virginia Beach. I popped the tape in, and in the midst of the music, we heard you start to bark, Yum Yum! The music was playing softly when I heard your quiet bark in the background. Bert and I looked at each other and laughed aloud. "That's Charlye! Play it again!" There are about five of your large barks there, Charlye. Amazing! Strong, powerful, as if you were saying "Go get 'em tomorrow, Bert. I know you'll do ok." It was brilliant, Charlye, and made us smile and laugh.

We knew then, that Bert's presentation would be absolutely brilliant, because the strength of your voice and bark coming at us that way meant you were with us.

There should be one other tape around, Charlye, with your voice on it. It's a tape of me playing the organ for Bert and I'm sure you bark at some point on it. When I find it, I'll take them both to the radio station and have them make one continuous fifteen minute tape of your barking.

It was great to hear you, dearest Charlye.

Earlier, we'd passed a huge truck bearing the name of the "Shaffer Trucking Company," from Omaha, Nebraska. We both felt our parents were with us. Have you met them yet, Charlye?

The wind is beautiful, the sun is strong, the flowers are coming into strength and bloom. It's a most beautiful time of the year and I sob at your absence. We shared the opening of Spring together throughout your fourteen years, Yum Yum. I cannot yet bear to look at the beauty and strength of the azaleas coming into bloom, without sobbing at the thought of you. This was our most beautiful time to walk together. Everyone said, "Charlye walks you."

Well, back to our trip to Detroit. We arrived about 11:00 P.M. and could not find a hotel within the general area of the General Motors Building. We stopped at a gas station, where we found a local police officer who led us in the direction of the downtown Days Inn. We felt that was your doing, Charlye. Since your death, we've felt you've been leading us toward motels which cater to pets—to Charlyes!

April 9, 1988

It's Saturday morning, dearest Charlye, and as I read what I wrote yesterday, I think of the hotels and motels we've been stopping in. I wonder, are you telling us we should have taken you more often? Or are you saying, "See, I'm with you!" We are passing through this eighth day of Passover. I didn't even share a piece of Matzoh with you. This opening of Spring, this sense of newness is oh, so painful, without you, Charlye. If I look upon you as being within the celebration of life and its new beginnings for your spiritually, I should smile, not cry. I guess I cry in selfishness. I can't touch you or hug you. It seems funny, too, that for the past several months I'd been telling Bert you were seeming more like a person each day, in your understanding of me and mine of you.

Now that your outer self is no longer here, dear Charlye, I sometimes wonder if, in my amazement of you, your love and your understanding, I sometimes took you for granted.

We didn't realize you had kidney problems. During that last month, you'd go to the office door or front door or patio door and bark to be let out. Sometimes I just wasn't conscious of your need, and you'd walk away. Then I'd call you back, you'd go to the door again, and we'd go outside.

You know, Charlye, there were so many things I wanted for you, and I got most of them. I never asked for your death, though, and in my own way that has tortured me. In fact, I thought I was protecting you against your death when I left Mother's bed jacket and blanket as protection for you.

When we left on this trip, we left the lights and TV on in the bedroom, just as we'd done when your earthly self were here. It was a good feeling to walk into the house, see your pictures and the light, and hear the sound of the TV. I wonder, in your spiritual self, can you go with us and yet, at the same time, still be here?

All kinds of vignettes flow, dear Charlye:
I now have to pick up any crumbs that fall to the floor, as there's no Charlye to help me.

I can now leave the dishwasher open as I load it with the dirty dishes, without having to say, "No, Charlye, you can't eat that dirty food."

I see you sitting on one of the leather chairs, as you are in your last photos. What gifts you've left me, dearest Charlye. One photo shows you in your familiar pose in the chair. In another, your eyes seem to follow me, just as they did when you watched me working. I'm sorry I always seemed to be working. I always thought you knew I loved you because we spent so much time together. Yet now I feel I should have taken more time to love you.

The vignette of sitting on the bench outside the kitchen, holding you as Bert drove away...We'd say, "Bye, Bert."

April 10, 1988

The vignette of me holding you by your tail as Bert pulled into the driveway, so you wouldn't run to him until he had stopped the car and was getting out. You still did that even during that last week before you died, dear Charlye.

Dear Charlye, no matter what they told me, I thought there was tomorrow, that I would always have tomorrows with you. We took care of you, bathed you, watched over you, kissed you, loved you. We always felt you would walk through life with us in your earthly self. It was our greatest joy to come home at night or to surprise you during the day. We'd find you sleeping, wake you up to a big hug and you'd kiss us, jump off the bed and run to the kitchen. Even during that last week. You looked like a baby, sleeping so tightly curled on our bed, with one leg and paw under your head. It gave us joy to look at you, and to hug you as you awakened.

Yesterday, dear Charlye, was the tenth Saturday since your last one. It was the Saturday I came home in mid-afternoon to spend an hour with you before having to go back to the Civic Center. I should have known you were sick. I should have been more patient, instead of saying, "Hurry, Charlye, let's go!" You didn't come to the kitchen door when I left; you just went back to your bed, so I went to you and told you I was leaving.

Oh, Charlye, who would have thought that a mere ten weeks later I'd be buying a beautiful yellow rose bush called "Caramel Creme," to plant in your honor and memory, between the bushes planted for my mother and father? Who would have thought that January 30th would be our last Saturday together? It hurts, Yum Yum, it hurts!

Bert so wanted a rose for you, that I bought the most beautiful, strongest-looking, yellow bush I could find. On our way home with it, I felt you were in the car with us. As I rolled the window down a wee bit, I felt you "smelling the wind."

Bert was so anxious to plant the rose bush, he did it this morning. Who would have thought there would, so soon, be a third rose between the two planted for my parents? Dearest Charlye, who would have thought?

Brad and Bert have been cleaning the back deck and the swimming pool for Spring and the onset of Summer. That's painful for both of us without you. How you loved to go in and out the patio door! You'd go out, feel the sun on your body until it got too warm, go back inside to cool off, then, five minutes later, you'd want to go back out again. You used to begin breathing heavily and I'd worry that you'd gotten too warm. I loved having you outside with us, and having you sit or lie by our legs on the chaise lounge. This Spring is terribly painful, dearest Charlye, without you here to enjoy it with us.

Charlye on chaise lounge

Would your death have hurt us less had you died in the cold of winter or in the midst of a bitter storm? I probably would have said, "I guess it's better he's not here. This cold was too painful for him." To have you die in the newness of Spring, though, hurts terribly, Charlye.

We still have the long foam pillows you slept on. I think I'll tell Bert tomorrow that we should discard them. I looked first to see if they had any of your hairs on them, but the breeze from the window had blown them all away.

I've been sitting in your leather chair in the living room, too. I found one hair yesterday. We can now wear all the navys and blacks we want, dear Charlye, without having to worry about brushing dog hairs off.

Bert asked me yesterday morning, "Are you making coffee for me this morning?" I said, "Well, I'm not making it for Charlye." We laughed, Charlye, and that's how we both want to live with our thoughts of you. We want to laugh, to smile...not to hurt.

Did I tell you how good it was, when we returned from Detroit this week, to come home and find the lights on and the television going in the bedroom, just as when you were here? I didn't have pain as I walked in, dear Charlye. Did you "walk in" with us, or did you get home ahead of us, Yum Yum?

Funny thing, Charlye, since you died I now make the bed in our bedroom. Bert always used to do it, but now that you and I no longer go out together, I make it, instead. Thanks for this added responsibility!

Zodie Stier said I'd find gifts from you all the time, so I always look for the spot where your nails cut into the blanket. I love it and am grateful, so there's some compensation in making the bed. As I write this, I'm wearing Mother's bed jacket. I'd never have taken it away from you, for I felt it was my insurance for your protection. Now I wear it almost every night!

April 11, 1988

The house is being painted, dear Charlye, and we're throwing away a lot of things. Your death made me realize nothing is here forever, so I'd better discard what we no longer need or use, before someone else does it for me.

If you saw us moving the furniture around, you'd probably be just as nervous as you were the week before we left Virginia Beach. You walked around the house all night, and no matter how I held you, I couldn't comfort you. In a way, I feel a little guilty. Did you think you lived in a mess? Anyway, since you didn't like the smell of nail polish, you probably wouldn't like the smell of the paint, either.

Last night, as I was cleaning up the back office and putting photo albums away, about five pictures of our rose garden fell out. They must have been taken about August of 1984 when we came back from Ghana. The roses for my parents bloomed strong and tall and in one picture you're between those two rose bushes, like a shadow. Who could have known that four short years later, your shadow would be replaced by a young, strengthening rose bush, planted in your memory?

Charlye

Dearest Charlye, I didn't understand the warnings. I assumed you would always be here. After all, I'd taken you to the doctor the last week in December and he'd given you a clean bill of health. Dearest Charlye, I'm sorry. I guess it was your time to go, but I didn't want to know.

Sometimes, on my way home, I begin to think maybe you've been away on vacation and I'll find you back. Then I realize that's not so. I began sobbing while telling this to Bert, but he said "yes," that you are away on vacation and I will see you later. It saddened me to realize-that could be 20-30 years from now. Then I thought that maybe, where you are, there's no concept of time, so I hope I find my reality, dear Charlye. You were here, but you had to go. This has been different from any of the times you were sick. No matter what the problem, you'd always recovered and returned home. This time it's different.

Bert just said I don't have to wait 20-30 years. I can feel you spiritually any time I want.

Dear Charlye, fourteen years ago today we left the boat we were painting in Patchogue, Long Island, went to the Bide A Wee Home in Bar Harbor, Long Island, and picked you out. We took you home in a little box and you became our "Charlye." You lived with us in Queens, New York; Stamford, Connecticut; Virginia Beach; and here in Prattville. You've ridden back with us to visit in Virginia Beach; you've gone to Daytona Beach with us. We took you wherever we could, dear Charlye, and felt good and proud to have you with us. Now you're gone, and we have to wait for you to take us with you.

Somehow, dearest Charlye, your spirit is with me and with us. I don't feel as lonely as I used to. Are you in my pockets? Are you walking with me? I know your eyes watch me from your marvelous picture.

I didn't write yesterday, Charlye, because I was racing around in the morning. Of course, I'd intended to write at night, but that didn't happen either. Still, you were with us all day, dear Charlye.

What revelations in our meeting with Dr. Hill, but you must know about these already. What your death has unleashed in understanding and awareness! Intellectually, I know you're no longer hurting, Charlye, and I'm sorry I didn't know how much you were hurting before. I know you're in a better place now and, spiritually, you're more with me than ever before. I must know that Charlye, and I must accept it.

I started this morning's writings by putting nail polish on two fingers. Then I smiled, remembering how you'd always turn your head away so definitively whenever you smelled nail polish. Did you do it spiritually this time?

Oh, Charlye, I've cried so much I sometimes don't even feel the tears running down my face. Please help me stop crying, and instead only smile when I talk or think about you.

I felt so complete with the three of us together. You and Bert and me...we were a family. I loved going to sleep at night knowing most of the time you were there on the bed all night. It was good, it was comforting. I loved coming home at night or running in, in the middle of the day. You were always there and so excited to see me or us. Perhaps you're more here now, because spiritually you can run with us.

I used to wonder where we'd be able to walk, with all the houses being built around here. More of the lots have "For Sale" signs on them since Spring has blossomed, dear Charlye. I don't have to worry about that now. I don't have to say, "No, Charlye, we can't walk here, somebody lives here." All these worries have evaporated now, Charlye.

Hi, dearest Charlye. The other day I put some bread crumbs alongside the wooden border where your roses are. I'd just begun my morning prayers today, when suddenly a blue jay swooped down, took one piece, and flew off with it. I felt as if it were you, saying, "Hello."

I'm amazed that, since you died it hurts to not see you, yet I don't feel as lonely as I did when you were here. I can't explain this phenomenon, unless perhaps you're walking with me all the time now. When I was away from you, we used to wonder: Well, which room is Charlye sleeping in now? Or, Mrs. Byrd is there with him, or Brad is coming in? Now we don't think that way. Now I feel you're with me and, while I still hurt, in a sense I feel complete. Does that make sense, Charlye?

Last night we had dinner at Shoney's to celebrate the anniversary of your arrival into our lives and hearts in 1974. The tears suddenly began to trickle down by cheeks. At times, this happens and I'm not even aware of it.

We've had one of our plants since 1967. I bought it near my mother's in the Bronx shortly after I bought the house in Queens. I find it interesting to own a green plant, which now almost reaches the ceiling, and which is older than you were. It came into the Queens' house seven years before you did. It's been in the hallway of every house we've lived in except in Virginia Beach, where it stood in the window by the kitchen. In the house in Connecticut it stood in the window at the foot of the steps. When we came home from work, you'd run down the steps and you and that plant would be waiting for us at the window. We would see you, first through the upstairs balcony; then, as you heard the car, you'd run down the stairs to wait for us.

It's always been a joy to come home and find you waiting for us, even when you'd be sound asleep and we gently waken you with hugs. It was always an exciting feeling to know you'd sometimes waited for us in the living room. I felt you had an internal clock that gave you a sense of when our workday was over, and that you'd come to the living room to wait, just so you'd be closer to the front door.

It's funny, dear Charlye, I now even have a chair in the living room, just like Bert. When you were here, I felt every chair in here was yours and I'd be sitting either in your chair or in the one you wanted. So I never really identified with a particular chair. Now I feel I do have my own chair, and have even left a few magazines near it. In a sense, you've "moved over," and given me a place. Thank you, dear Charlye.

Yesterday, Bert said, "He was the most magnificent dog in the world." I don't see you as a dog, but as "my Charlye!"

April 15, 1988

Dearest Charlye, I was anxious to get to work this morning, so am only now sitting down to talk to you. Did I tell you that we had a meeting yesterday at work? It began at 7:00 P.M. and about 7:15, I got a tear in my eye when I realized I didn't have to worry about whether or not you were O.K. Everything seems so easy now, but how it hurts.

It's also Friday night and, once again, I have that feeling like a hole in my chest at the prospect of another weekend without you. It's not as bad as it was, though, Charlye, and for that I'm grateful.

Your rose bush is strong and tough-looking, and has four buds on it. I've put some bread crumbs around it and am hoping the birds will collect them tomorrow.

Yesterday was the 14th and it was the first Thursday I've awakened and not thought about it being ten weeks since your body left us. Every time I think of that I choke up and want to sob. Ten weeks seems such a short time and yet, put in terms of seventy days, it seems much longer. I remember I couldn't wait for the first Thursday to pass. I had thought my ache would diminish; instead, it grew worse and worse. Tomorrow will be the 11th Saturday, dear Charlye, and I can't wait until fifty-two of them have passed. Hopefully, by then, I'll be able to laugh with you, about you, rather than choking up.

That first Saturday after you died, you came to me ever so strongly, and slept in the crook of my arm. I felt you so intensely that I was afraid to move. I wish you could come back to me that way at least once a month. Is that possible, Charlye?

I still miss you as I clean up the kitchen. Invariably, I'd drop a piece of cheese or such on the floor while preparing meals, and you'd look for it. If I served Bert in the living room, you'd jump off your chair to get a nibble from him. When you were here, you were around us all the time, and I loved it. I loved your presence. It seems like I have so much time now, and yet, though we must have spent much time together, I feel I didn't spend much time with you at all.

From Christmas until the day you died I kept a kitchen chair in the living room, right next to your chair. I wanted to be able to touch you as I sat there with you. I put the chair back in the kitchen the day you died. Now I sit in your chair or the other leather chair. I keep trying to find more of your hairs, but there are fewer and fewer of them. Who would have thought there would be no more of them around? I'm looking for a locket to put in some of your hair and a picture, which I can then wear around my neck. Maybe then I'll feel better.

You know we are now on daylight saving time, so the clock is set an hour ahead. I no longer wake up in that state of panic at 4:40 A.M., the time of day you died. It's too complicated, now, to figure out when it is, and for this I'm grateful. I still can't bear to keep an alarm clock next to my bed. To see the time reminds me of getting up practically every half hour those last two evenings you were alive. I'd hurt so terribly for you, yet didn't know what to do to help you.

You're better now, Charlye, or so they all tell me, including our medium, who connected with you. She said you told her to, "Tell my mommy I love her."

"Tell her I had to go, my legs were hurting." Dear Charlye, I treated you as a human being and since you really didn't complain, though you might wimper a bit when Bert touched you, I still can't accept that you're better off! I guess I'm just selfish. Good Night, dear Charlye, until tomorrow!

Hi, Yum Yum. It's a beautiful, healthy, sunny day and your rose plant and its buds look so strong. The buds on my mother's bush are beginning to open and the color is a pinkish-red. That bush has many smaller buds on it.

It's funny, Charlye, but when Bert went to sleep last night I didn't feel alone. I was writing to you and felt complete. Normally, when he'd go off to sleep, I'd get a terrible ache of loneliness. Somehow, with you as a spirit, I feel you must be with me at all times. That ache of general loneliness no longer comes over me. I look at your picture, where your eyes follow me as they did when you were here, and I love it. What a gift you have left me! How did you do it, Charlye? I just stare at it, thinking of you, and your whole body and spirit awaken for me.

As springtime approached and we began to see the beauty of the Azaleas opening up, I just sobbed missing you and the Spring walks we shared. The newness of Spring, the brightness of the day, the warmth, the clear sun...all hurt so much without you. We loved springtime together and I cried bitterly that you weren't here for this one. You should have waited to share springtime with me. I can't bear to walk the same paths we took together, so if I do go walking, I take a different route. I think of you as I walk, and hold my head high, smelling the wind. Sometimes I come back with tears but, lately, I've tried to come back with fewer tears and more smiles.

When you were little and we had to leave you, I'd pay for the largest cage in the Connecticut veterinarian's office, but when I'd take you there how you cried, and cried. I didn't understand, then, dear Charlye. Do you forgive me?

One other time you cried bitterly. Oh, dear Charlye, how stupid of me! We were still in Connecticut. You were under the desk in the library and when you stood up, you started to limp. It was late at night, I panicked, and we ran to an emergency clinic in Norwalk. The stupid doctor, if he were a doctor, stuck a needle in you, for what I don't know, but how you screamed and screamed. The next day, we took you to Davis Animal Clinic, where the vet said there was nothing wrong with your leg. Now that you're not here, I hurt for that stupid mistake of mine. How an over-anxious parent can kill a child!

Those are the only times feel I've felt I really hurt you, dearest Charlye. I've not forgotten, but I hope you have.

I was shopping in Food World yesterday and when I passed the dog bones, I choked up. It was always fun to shop, call you from the kitchen as I came into the house, and say, "Charlye, I have a present for you." It was a delicious feeling to know you were happy and that you were as excited to get a present, as I was eager to buy it for you.

When we came home last night, I asked Bert to please drive around the top part of the hill, so we could see some of the building taking place up there. I choked up and won't do that again. That's where you and I always walked and I can't bear to take that path again.

In the past year, when I'd bought you bones, you never seemed to like the first one I'd take out. I'd have to put out a few of them, and then let you take your pick.

I'd also had the feeling that maybe your mouth was hurting, so you couldn't chew them the way you wanted. You'd twist the bone around in your mouth for awhile, but then put it down. You'd begun doing that with your food, too, Charlye. Was it hurting, dear Charlye, without my realizing?

As I look back, I realize how much I expected from you. I even expected you to talk. I somehow took it for granted. Since you'd just look at me and say nothing, I guess I just "pushed you on" to do the things we'd been doing together. When you couldn't jump on the bed anymore, you told me, and I lifted you up. I guess I expected you to say, "I hurt," and when you didn't, I just expected us to go on the way we always had.

I'm grateful you didn't die in Dr. Jones' office during those last three days, when you were there for intravenous feedings. Had he told us you could stay home, I'd have stayed home with you. Intellectually, I know it was your time, but still it hurts. There's almost no reason to come home anymore, other than to sleep, so we're straightening up and repainting, so it'll be pleasant and relaxing. I need to be surrounded by you and have pictures of you all around the house.

When I find myself thinking perhaps you're only away, and that when I get home I'll find you've returned, Bert brings me back to reality. He tells me, "Charlye is not coming back," and I realize that's true. When I'm getting dressed in the morning, I throw my clothes on the bed and don't worry about getting dog hairs on them. There are no more dog hairs to get on anything, dearest Charlye. Even the ones on the bed are flying away, except those few left on the purple blanket. I try to sleep with the corner of that blanket, where I think your toenail or teeth may have pulled into it one day. I don't think I'll ever wash that blanket. Most nights I also sleep with Mother's bed jacket, which I used to put around you and never wanted to take away from you.

How I loved the changing of the seasons with you! If we went out of town and left you at home, I felt much better if the weather were nice. It hurt to leave you and I didn't want you out in rain and bad weather with someone else. We sometimes even walked at a shopping mall, so we'd be protected and, recently, I'd held the umbrella over you to keep you dry.

April 18, 1988

Dearest Charlye, we left the house early this morning, so I write to you tonight-as I lie in bed next to your picture. Your urn is on the dresser, next to Nancy Bone's flowers, which are a perfect complement to the color of your urn. We had a dinner party last night in Nancy's honor, to celebrate her recent marriage. Zodie and Bul Stier attended, along with Elliott, the Mims, Nancy's new in-laws, and Rubye and Tom Kennedy. Rubye was thoughtful enough to put a condolence note about your death in the Business and Professional Women's Club newsletter. It warmed our hearts in thoughtfulness and love, dearest Charlye.

As I was cooking for the company this morning, I played one of the tapes with your voice on it; Bert and I were just sad and crying. Usually, when I'd work in the kitchen, you'd be under my feet. I'd have to sternly say, "No, Charlye," if you tried to grab a piece of food which had fallen on the floor, but which wasn't good for you.

As the sun came out, and the day wore on, Bert and I were sitting in the living room. He asked if the picture of you in the living room could be moved to the top of the television set. I said, "Yes," while hanging on to my heart, dearest Charlye. But by putting it there, the people standing in line to enter the dining room all saw you kind of in line, too. Bert and I knew you were at that dinner party, Yum Yum, and we both felt wonderful. It was a lovely afternoon and evening once we recognized and felt the "presence of your company" with us.

The dinner party for Nancy was the first one we'd had since you died, Yum Yum, and it seemed fitting it should be for her. She took care of you most of the time when we were away.

It's raining bitterly and the thunder is tremendous. That's the only time I can rationalize, I'm glad you're not here to "walk in the rain." I used to worry that you'd catch cold.

Good-night, dearest Charlye. I'm falling asleep on you!

Sunday mornings hurt, dearest Charlye. They're easier in that I can sleep later since I don't have to walk you. It seems I have more time these days, yet I don't think I spent much extra time with you. At night, we seem to fall asleep in the living room chairs. When you were here, we'd stay awake, talk with you, and have conversations. Your death has made me aware of our own mortality, dear Charlye.

I wonder...did I ever wonder, did it ever cross my mind...if we should die before you, who would take care of you? I think years ago I must have thought about that, but it hadn't crossed my mind in recent years. I just thought we'd all be together, always, and that we'd die together. Now you're there ahead of us, but hopefully you'll know us when we get there.

It was raining fiercely yesterday, dearest Charlye, and your roses are beginning to open up. I feel alive with them, as if a part of you is on earth. I'm trying to teach the birds that if they want bread crumbs, they have to go near your roses to get them.

I look at the notes I write from time to time to use when I'm putting my thoughts here. April 5th we left for Detroit but I hated leaving. We left the TV on as usual, grasped your urn and looked at your pictures. Spiritually, I felt you'd be coming with us. I left Mother's bed jacket on my bed.

Some mornings I feel so heavy. Who would have thought I'd be looking at your picture, writing about and to you in the early morning, instead of taking you for your first walk of the day? Sometimes I even got the sand out of your eyes in the morning. It felt so good. Like a baby you waited, and then wagged your tail when I was finished.

While in Detroit, we experienced high winds and I held my head high, "smelling the wind." During our drive there, we heard your bark, loud and clear, on one of our audio tapes. Amidst the tears, we laughed and felt better.

When we first come home at night it hurts, dearest Charlye, but then we get into our nightly routine. We also tend now to doze or fall asleep, perhaps to avoid the pain of your absence.

When I come home and I've misplaced my house keys, like I did when you were here, I call you to help me find them, and "we" find them, Charlye. Remember when you'd need to go out and I'd say,"Charlye, I can't find my keys." I'd look and look, then I'd find them and show them to you. You'd wag your tail and we'd be on our way out.

There were so many things we did together, Charlye.

Who would have thought Barri's Stanley Kaplan notebook, used almost 20 years ago, would be in use again today to write and talk to my Charlye?

April 20, 1988

Hi, dearest Charlye. It's 8:30 A.M. and I've been up since about 4:30 A.M. That's something I've not often done since you died. I couldn't bear to get up early and work without you next to me. Now, with daylight savings time and everything, the clock is all mixed up, so I don't look at it as anything more than time...time to do or not do something.

There was much paperwork to clean up from the business, so I figured I'd get into it this morning. I had your picture facing me, your eyes right on top of me. That was a good feeling for work, and I didn't feel alone. I wanted to touch your picture and stroke you. Sometimes I blow at your picture, the way I used to blow in your face. You'd turn your head, then suddenly come back for more. It was a fun game for us.

It's no fun now to go home in the middle of the day. You're not here for us to surprise, so we just get our work done and move on.

On our way to Detroit, we stopped at a Cracker Barrel Restaurant. We both choked up, remembering the times we'd taken you to the Cracker Barrel in Montgomery. We'd park the car right up front so we could look out the big window and see you looking back at us. We found such pleasure, fun and warmth with you.

One of the last business trips we took by car was to Omaha, Nebraska in June of 1987. You were there to greet us when we returned, dearest Charlye. When we left for Detroit, Bert and I were crying and reminiscing. We grasped your urn and just left. It's going to be painful around the pool this summer, too. You'd finally reached the point of coming right to the edge of the pool, and letting me kiss you while I was in the pool. I always felt good about that because it showed how much you trusted me. When you were younger, you'd let me take you into the pool, but after your legs were operated on, I was afraid to do that. We always enjoyed being outside together, but I try not to think about that now. I just go about my business, and do what I have to do.

Snuggling with Caroline

Spring time brings a sense of newness we loved to share together. This new newness hurts without your presence. Your death closed a chapter for us.

Today is the beginning of the 11th week since your death, dearest Charlye. We went to the Mexican Restaurant last night and I suddenly started to choke up. I was thinking about you, about Thursday being the 11th week, and about that sad night 11 weeks ago, when we brought you home to die.

After you died, I moved the telephone from my side of the bed to Bert's. While you were here, I felt I had to over-compensate in my relationship with Bert to make up for spending so much time with you. I'm more relaxed now, dearest Charlye, and I no longer feel Bert feels he is "number 2" in my feelings. I don't have to over-compensate for anything, and I no longer jump when the phone rings.

Do you remember the pretty aqua jogging suit I'd bought to wear for our morning walks, dearest Charlye? I'd gotten it only a few months (it feels more like moments) before you died.

In the years we traveled together in the yellow Cadillac, my CB handle was "Charlye's Momma." Charlye's Momma would be asked to meet "Marijuana Joe" on the beach at Virginia Beach! As I'd drive home from Washington, D.C. to Virginia Beach, those CB conversations kept me awake.

Then I'd come into the house, and you'd rush to greet me. What delicious feelings, Charlye! It was wonderful to rush into the house, wherever we were living, and have you rush to greet us. If you were asleep on our bed, we'd wake you with a big hug. "Charlye, your Mommy's home." You'd get all excited and jump off the bed. Bert used to make fun. "Look at all the lipstick on your face, Charlye," and we'd smile.

The only time I'm grateful for and can really rationalize your absence is when it's raining.

Good morning, dearest Charlye. I'm so tired these mornings. Last night I came home and choked up about you, Yum Yum, and in the morning Bert was feeling lonely and blue.

I now keep this book in the dresser (night table) next to my bed, along with some of my mother's letters and things. Just now, as I pulled it out to write to you, the pretty pink and beige chiffon scarf I'd given my mother years ago, pulled out with it. I remembered the day we found it under the dining room table. You'd been playing with it and had torn it. We sewed the torn edges, and I've always saved it. It's another memory of you, and I felt it was another way you were saying, "Hello."

I love finding mementoes of you or from you. It's as if you're coming by or "dropping in" just to say, "Hello." Or are you always with us, Yum Yum?

At times, I jump rope right near your rose bush, and pull the weeds crowding out your "territory." I often feel, as I stand near your roses, that they wave in the wind, while all the other leaves and flowers are still. Though I look intently at the others, I feel they're not living, while yours are. It's as if you're waving your tail, saying "Hello."

April 30, 1988

Dearest Charlye, Mrs. Spencer from Virginia Beach wrote us a beautiful note expressing her sympathy. The card read "Thinking of you and Caring." Your picture's in her bedroom and she looks at you everyday, too. Her letter was exquisite and made me sob. She wrote that you knew how much we loved you, which made us feel good, Yum Yum. I've attached a copy of my response to her.

April 30, 1988

Dear Mrs. Spencer: It was so good to hear from you and to know you had a beautiful birthday party.

I hope the enclosed gets to you so you don't have to worry about cashing it. I felt so good that as always you asked about our Charlye. The enclosed picture was taken December 19, 1987, less than 7 weeks later he would no longer be here. Who could believe that from the picture? He died of kidney failure February 4, 1988 at 4:35 a.m. in bed with us—and that's a gift from God to have someone you so love die in bed with you. We thought you would like this beautiful last photograph taken.

We had like five days "notice." On Monday night I was told "he is sick." Tuesday, very sick. Wednesday, terminal...and so he couldn't stay anymore.

Our hearts have been terribly, terribly broken, but we're learning not to cry and to smile and laugh when we talk about him. He was cremated, and his ashes are in our bedroom with us.

We love you and think about you—I have put your letter asking about Charlye next to his picture.

Our love,
Carol, Bert

Please take care of yourself.

88

May 1, 1988

Dearest Charlye, I didn't write this morning because I went to a meeting "which didn't exist where I had gone." I went to the Montgomery Chamber of Commerce, when I should have gone to Selma. It's been a successful day, though. I believe we're going to settle on some property, a beautiful location, for the new building. We'd always said we'd put a large, magnificent photo of you in it, but deep down I worried about that. I know you didn't like to be left alone in our work place, so I don't know yet what I'm going to do. I think you'd love it, Yum Yum. It will be brightly lit, and the sun and light will always shine on you.

I've been putting bread crumbs out for the birds, near your rose bush. Today I brought home the roll I didn't finish at Wendy's to give to them. I used to bring napkins home from Wendy's for you, so it seemed symbolic to bring home bread from there to put near your rose bush. Perhaps, as the birds soar high, your spirit comes closer. I love talking about you. It takes away the ache of crying. I smile more these days, rather than cry, and for that I'm grateful, dear Charlye.

Last night we went to a dinner at the Synagogue. A young lady sat at our table, and she'd heard me speak the previous morning. I had mentioned you in my address, as I always try to do, and she said I had touched a sadness in her. She has a 14 year-old dog who is ill, and I shared our pain with her and suggested she take her dog to see Dr. Jones.

Did I tell you that as I was going to get the mail the other evening, a little bug jumped in front of me? I thought about how you used to stare as a frog or toad jumped and how I'd hold you back so it wouldn't jump in your face.

The other day, I put on my blue bathrobe, which always used to be covered with your hairs. No hairs now, dearest Charlye. I'm beginning to accept that and when Bert and I find a hair we smile and ask each other, "Is it Charlye's or is it

89

Carol's?" Your's is silkier than mine, Yum Yum, with a touch of brown/black at the end, while mine has a little bend to it because of its kinky texture.

I was in a B. Dalton Bookstore today and bought a few books on dogs, to help give me some background for writing. One is John Steinbeck's "Travels with Charlie." He spells Charlye differently than we did. Another of the books, "Dog Watching," explains why dogs bark, wag their tails, and all that. Still another contains poems about dogs, written by people who have lost their pets. I don't know why I never thought about such books before. I guess because I thought you and I basically understood each other. It's interesting to read these and see how they explain some of our interpretations of each other. Some of the explanations offered coincide with what I'd felt about you in a natural setting. After reading some of them, I didn't feel badly about not having the book while you were here.

Hi, Yum Yum, it's Mother's Day. I never thought about it when you were here because the three of us were together and I felt so complete. Now I have reminders of you in a locket I wear around my neck, and that feels great, Yum Yum. Your rose bush seems limp, so Bert put the sprinklers on yesterday and hopefully now it will awaken with the proper fertilizers when we had planted it. There are three buds on it, but they've not yet opened fully. One bud, which seems stronger than the others, will, I hope, Yum Yum.

Did you see that little piece of hair I clipped on to yesterday's writing page, Yum Yum? A few weeks ago I found one of your hairs in the living room, (I wrote you about it) and put it in the peanut dish. Well, yesterday, I was eating peanuts from that dish and that hair got in my mouth, just as they sometimes used to when I'd kiss you. I've saved that piece of hair, Charlye.

We left for Monroeville directly from work. We didn't have to be concerned about going home first, or leaving you behind, so we just picked up and went. When we arrived in Monroeville, we had dinner at a charming little deli owned by a young woman. We spent the entire time talking about you. Here it's been three months since your death and I'd bought the locket to put your hair and photo in. We were missing you and felt sad talking about you. Neither of us had felt this way even when our parents died, but they had a specific place in our lives: they were our parents. They had certain roles and responsibilities to us and for us, and we did things both for and with them.

It was different with you, Charlye. You had no "place," per se, but were rather all over. You were part of everything we did. Even when we bought a van for the business, we thought about how much you'd love, and it was fun to put you in it. We couldn't go anywhere unless we'd taken care of you first. You were part of everything we did, Yum Yum. You were all over, so your "place" was every place. That's why your leaving hurts all over. We love you, Yum Yum, and we always will. We learned so much from you, in life and in death, and every day we continue to learn from your earthly presence and your spirititual presence.

The neighborhood kittens come visiting now, and look in the patio window. I wonder if they're looking for you, Yum Yum. We left some milk and bread out for them and it was gone this morning, so they must have been hungry. A squirrel was nibbling on the tape of the swimming pool cover this morning, too, so Bert went out and shooed him away.

May 9, 1988

Dearest Charlye, so much has happened today. At 1:45 this morning, the Prattville police rang our doorbell and said we had a car in the ditch in Letohatchee. As we were dashing out of the house, my first thoughts were about not having to explain it to you. You didn't have to worry about us running out of the house so soon after having gone to bed. You're being well taken care of now, dearest Charlye, and yet our first thoughts were still about you.

Did I tell you we went to Birmingham Saturday, to the funeral of Ruth Bradshaw's mother? It was a beautiful, uplifting service and I thought of you throughout. I hope by now you have introduced yourself to Mrs. Hill, Ruth's mother, dearest Charlye. Please also introduce her to my folks, Yum Yum, and to Moeder and her husband.

I listened to the well-known astrologist, Linda Goodman tonight. She commented that she doesn't believe in time, other than as a concept for organization and boundary. That's nice to extend our lives together that way, dearest Charlye. It makes the difference between us easier to bear, Yum Yum. If there's no measurement, we will see each other sooner. I'm exhausted now, but I'll write more tomorrow.

I came back to the house about 4:30 P.M. What a sadness, Yum Yum, to come into the house in the middle of a beautiful, sunny day, and find you not here. I want to sob, dear Charlye, and yet you're so funny. I was eating some fruit salad in the kitchen, in front of your picture, when I dropped a couple pieces of fruit on the floor. They landed right in front of your picture and I just looked at them and smiled. I didn't have to say "No" as you'd look at it on the floor and perhaps decide to "go for it." What a tease, Yum Yum! There was no reason for you to make this happen, but I loved it and it turned my tears to a smile.

Did you arrange, Yum Yum, for Dr. Sayre and his wife to have dinner with us tonight? That was nice. We talked about you and about the psychic aura of dogs. Your's is ever so strong. I showed Dr. Sayre my locket, containing your hair and photo. You're still in the middle, between Bert and me, Yum Yum. I love it and I love you.

You know, if I'm hurriedly getting dressed for work, I leave the plastic from the cleaners and a hanger in the waste paper basket. I look at them and say, "I don't have to worry Charlye will hurt himself." I think of you each time I do something differently than we'd done together. I recognize your earthly body isn't here, and how I wish your spiritual body would come to me and touch me at night, Yum Yum.

Ruth Washington's brother-in-law from New York died early Saturday morning, Charlye. Will you meet him? You'll have a lot of people to introduce me to and, just as when you were here, you'll be the one leading the way. That's how I met many of our neighbors, Charlye.

May 11, 1988

Hi, dearest Charlye, another day away from the day you died. Tomorrow should be about the 13th week, Yum Yum, and we still hurt, we still cry, particularly when the sun shines strong and bright. We feel the warmth of your body, the gaze of your eyes, the strength of your bark, Yum Yum. I can't believe you're not coming back here. I keep looking at your picture, wishing you could walk out of it, yet knowing that's not possible.

My pattern of behavior has changed since you left. Now I get up and rush out the door to go to work; no Charlye to walk or spend time with. What pain, dearest Charlye.

Sunday Bert was washing the back patio with a hose, and some water came through onto your chair, the one we called "Charlye's chair." I could just picture you jumping off the chair, being a little angry at getting wet and giving Bert your "What's this?" look. I had to smile, Yum Yum. You'd have gotten the fun of it and probably come back for more, just as you'd come to the edge of the pool when I was in the water. In the beginning, you'd stay as far away as you could, but then you grew to trust me and you'd come right up to the water's edge. How I loved that, Yum Yum! Sometimes I'd touch you with my wet hands and you'd walk away...but you'd always come back.

Oh, Yum Yum, so many surprises from you this week. I found one of your dog bones under the toaster. What a magnificent Mother's Day gift. I think I told you I'd also found two of your bones in my desk at work. I've left them there and it's a wonderful feeling to open my desk and see them there!

Good night, Yum Yum.

May 12, 1988

Dearest Charlye, today marks the 13th week since your leaving and so many beautiful things happened! First, I took that music tape, "Reggae Music and Charlye" and asked the radio station person if he could extract your bark so I could hear it for about 15 minutes straight. It was marvelous, Yum Yum, marvelous. I was driving along, just listening to you bark. How I laughed, dearest Charlye. We had part of the tape of you barking at yourself.

May 13, 1988

Hi, dearest Charlye. We went to the Synagogue, Yum Yum, where we say our prayers for the dead. I always repeat your name and, because of you, we go to the Synagogue as often as we can. Our hearts are filled with you.

May 15, 1988

Dearest Charlye, I was so tired last night I hardly wrote to you, but tonight I feel more awake. As we were coming home last night, a car was being towed out of a ditch on a rural road near the house. A police car was standing nearby, and in a flash a "little Charlye" perked his head up, just like you used to, and was looking all around. It was so quick, dearest Charlye, the movements and all were just like you. I nearly asked Bert to stop the car, but I didn't. That split-second glance as we passed felt like a "Hello" from you, Yum Yum. It was a nice feeling and made me smile.

Bert and Elliott are repainting the last bedroom you were in. We're using a soft color, called "peach mimosa." The coloring of your hair blends into the room, Yum Yum, and I may put your poster portrait over the bed in there. I like that room for you anyway, dearest Charlye, and I bet I'd enjoy sleeping in there knowing you picture's over me. It's always felt good to relax in there. The sun was bright and you could look out the window. Dearest Charlye, who could have known that one day you'd be elevated from the bed to the wall? There are so many ways we make our place.

Hi, Charlye. I was just lying in bed thinking if you were here, with all this painting going on, you'd be walking around sniffing or turning your head away to express your dislike of the odor. That's what you'd do with the nail polish and it makes me smile now to think about it.

I'd hoped the moving of the furniture in order to paint wouldn't make you nervous, Yum Yum. Bert made fun last night, putting that stuffed animal door stopper between the bed pillows, so only the head was showing. If we looked at it quickly, it looked like you. All this make believe, Yum Yum! We smile and we cry.

If I sit in the living room and meditate over you, Yum Yum, that last week you were here hurts terribly. How I wish I could change it, how I wish I could have understood it and hugged you. The only thing that consoles me is knowing how happy you were with the chicken soup and rice we made for you. That, and writing to you, are the only things that keep me going.

I wish you'd come to me in the night sometimes, just as you did that first Saturday after you died. I love your locket and it feels good to have you so close. I remember in Queens I had a picture of you on my car visor. You were always my Charlye, Yum Yum. Always!

I have to smile now, when I've finished eating, and set my plate on the floor until I put it in the sink. Sometimes I put it down and say, "Gee, Charlye would have enjoyed licking this!" Things change, Yum Yum, movement of things we used to do…but you're always there, Yum Yum. You will always be loved!

Your rose bush hasn't done too well, but the buds were beautiful, so I've cut them and put them in your vase. Bert's started the irrigation system now, so maybe it'll rejuvenate the rose bush.

You know, by writing to you each day, I keep track of the date; otherwise, I wouldn't keep track. Even with this, you keep me in touch and in line, YumYum.

On May 3rd, Bert told me he'd dreamt about you on Miramar Lane in Stamford. He said you were standing near the tree where all the squirrels used to be, and you were wagging your tail. He said he was so happy watching you. He was reminiscing about the time you ran away from home, when my mother died. When they found you and brought you back, you proudly looked around as if to say, "I did it!" You never ran away again.

At this very moment (7:41 a.m.) a blue jay has landed on the patio bannister and looked into our bedroom. Did you just "send him" to say "Hello?"

Talk to you later, Yum Yum. We love you.

Dearest Charlye. We're so tired tonight, but I'll write tomorrow. We love you, dearest Charlye. It's so different without you here. We have accepted your death, and yet we still hurt terribly. We come home at night with a sense of loneliness and grief. It's almost as if we should come home just to go to bed, so we don't have to think. We're busy at work, and you're at work with us, as a gift to us. It's not the same at home, where your "place" was everywhere. Work had a certain boundary of presence, so when we're busy working we think of you as if in the present. When we're home we know our reality is but a dream.

You were all ours, and how we loved and treasured you.

Hi, Yum Yum. Today, for some reason, I sobbed terribly for you. Tomorrow it will be fourteen-weeks since your death, dear Charlye. That Wednesday night was so horrible.

Last night you finally came to me in my dreams. You were lying on my bed. I started to awaken, but didn't see you and worried that you'd gotten under the bed after I'd told you not to. Had you gotten so thin that you could get under the bed, or had you been locked in a closet, something which had never happened before. Then, as I awoke more fully, I remembered you had died, so I couldn't see your body to touch it. That's O.K., Yum Yum. If that's what had to be, and you had to die, I understand. I was so very grateful to have seen you in my dreams. I only wish it would happen more often.

Bert and I thought that since we'd taken your magnificent photo and put it in the bedroom you and I'd enjoyed so much for an afternoon nap, or for relaxing, you were probably happy we'd moved it there. You could look outside, or through the kitchen window, so we could see.you and you could see us, as we came in from outside.

I think you'll like being in that room. Like the Lord of the Manor you overlook all the entrances to the house. Who would've believed, Yum Yum, one day you'd be above the bed instead of on it? What else will happen that is new and unpredictable? Where else will be walk that you will have trod before in our lives? Dear Charlye, you're such a comfort, then and now.

The May 23rd issue of "Newsweek" contains an article entitled "How Smart are Animals?" I can tell them, Yum Yum, "How Smart My Charlye Was and Is." I somehow feel, Yum Yum, that you're my psychic spirit, the one that helps us achieve in every way possible and makes the work load lighter and more realistic. Dear Charlye, I feel that, in your heavenly state, you are our spirit and our leader under God. I feel you care and that you'll lead us to a more successful and easier path. Dear Charlye, I feel your sensitivities are stronger now than they've ever been. I feel your person and awareness of us is stronger than when your earthly body was here. I feel your humanness is all enriching and encompassing, dearest Charlye.

That room is bright and ever so pleasant with you in it, Yum Yum. I think your coming to me in my dreams is an example of "telling me" you like being there, too, Yum Yum.

Dearest Charlye, fourteen weeks ago today! Oh, Yum Yum, the hurt remains, but thank God the pain lessens. Your picture looks beautiful in the guest bedroom. It was our favorite room, with the sun coming in, feeling the carpet of the green grass. Today we go to Mobile, Charlye. I'll take the book and write much to you. Good night, dearest Yum Yum!

Hi again, dearest Charlye. I brought your letter book with me. We've come to Mobile to attend a two-day State of Alabama Women's Convention. Would I have gone had you been here, Yum Yum? I don't think about it. I just know that since you're not here, we go when we can, without thinking about it. Spiritually, I just hope you go with me wherever I go, Yum Yum. Maybe I'm less alone now, Yum Yum, because you're always with me.

I can't feel your weight on me anymore, Yum Yum, but I think and think about you. You're in the locket around my neck, close to my heart. I laugh when I hear the tape of your voice, but Bert cries, so I'll listen to it alone.

I talk about you often. I have our memories with Dr. Hill. I talk about how you'd overcome your fear of the pool, and learned to trust me enough to come right to the edge of the water. I thought that was just pure love and Dr. Hill saw it as the ultimate in trust. I just knew that we loved you, that you were pure joy, and that you loved everything we could possibly give you.

We have such delicious memories of watching you outside. It was no fun for us to be outside if you weren't with us watching, Yum Yum. Sometimes it was too warm and you'd go back inside, but then you'd sit in Bert's chair so you could continue to watch us. It was all joy, happiness and togetherness, Yum Yum. We'll smile and laugh, dear Charlye, but it'll never be the same.

I figured out, dearest Charlye, why the pain is so great, and the void and hole so large. You were all around us, all over the place with us. You were everywhere. How do we fill a void that's "one big everywhere?" A child has his or her place. If one loses a limb, one finds a substitute, a replacement. There's just no substitute for a pure love that was everywhere a part of us, Yum Yum. That's the difference.

The other day, I drove into the back part of the Deer Run area, up the back hill. The house frames you and I used to walk around are now completed homes, with people living in them. You were such a strong part of the area for me, Yum Yum, and how I worried that, as the houses got built, there would be no place left to walk you, or for you and I to walk together. Now you're not here to see all the houses completed or for us to walk. Somehow, though, I feel as if you've led us to put your picture in the guest room, Yum Yum. From there you can watch over us from all directions.

Once in a while I come into the house in the middle of the day, when the sun is shining brilliantly, and I ache for you, Yum Yum. Saturdays and Sundays, if we're home all day, are still rough without you, too. Both of us ache terribly. It seems we go out for dinner, go home, go to bed, and hope the ache has passed until morning. When the sun rises again, the fullness of your spirit is apparent in the brilliance of the day. It's now 10:30 P.M., Yum Yum. How you hated being in hotels with us!

May 20, 1988

You arer always with us spiritually, Yum Yum. Tonight at dinner, in this Mobile motel, we met Lula Davis of Bessemer and her friend, Lou Patton. They both had dogs they loved, too. Have you met them, or Lou Patton's late sister? As we meet more people, Yum Yum, we seek to share them with you. Does that give you more company?

Our room here overlooks the activity of Mobile Bay; draining the soil, barges, ships moving in the middle of the night. We wondered what it would've been like to walk you along the docks.

May 21, 1988

Hi, dearest Charlye. How we hate to go home. There's a sadness that overwhelms us as we head back from anywhere. We hate to go near the house because you're not there. We stopped off at Bul and Zodie's before we got to the house, and that gave us a sense of kinship. She mentioned Dee Dee, we mentioned Charlye, and then we went home.

As we pull into the driveway, get out of the car and approach the mailbox, your magnificent photo glows out from every window of the guest room, Yum Yum. We can see you from outside, and we pray that you can see and feel us, too. Then we go inside and your photo looks out into the hallway and all over, Yum Yum. You're in just about every room, just as you were all around and under foot most of the time. It makes us feel better.

As the end of the meeting this morning, I won a door prize, a lovely seashell-glazed dish. I felt it was a present from you, Yum Yum. It was a good meeting, and we'll go forth from there.

We love you, dearest Charlye. It's O.K. We're home now, surrounded by your pictures and urn. Good night, Charlye.

May 23, 1988

Hi, dearest Charlye. I thought of you, among other things, as I was driving home this evening. I saw you as you used to be, waiting for me at the window of our apartment in Arlington. As I'd run home to you at 3:15 in the afternoon, I'd see you from downstairs and call, "Charlye, I'm home." How happy we were to see each other! We'd take long walks together and I'd carry water for you because sometimes you'd get thirsty. It was just the two of us, Yum Yum, you and me, and I loved it. That was a rough summer for both of us, but I felt secure in that we were together. It was nice, too, to ride together in the yellow Cadillac from Virginia Beach to Arlington, and to stop at the rest area off 1-95. It was good just to be with you, Yum Yum.

When we were at the Stouffer Motel in Mobile, I thought of the Christmas we shared in Virginia. The three of us drove from Virginia Beach and met Barri and her family at the Marriot at Tyson's Corner. When we left you alone in the room, you were upset, but I felt good that we were all together. I always felt incomplete when you were away from us, Yum.Yum, and a holiday just wasn't a holiday if we were apart.

Hi, Yum Yum. I worked at home today and missed you terribly. I went to the post office this afternoon and missed having you with me. I didn't close the steel door when I left, but just locked the glass door. If you'd been here and not gone with me, you'd have been waiting for me behind that door and would have barked furiously when I returned. I'd have had to give you some food, a "Charlye" present.

Aunt Esther sent a beautiful picture of you that she'd taken in Virginia Beach. It must have been warm because you're panting and it looks as if you're walking back into the house to cool off. It's a great photo of you, Yum Yum, and is unlike any of the others I have.

One of our old gold towels, which we're had since before you were born, is lying over an outside chair. It's strange to think about that towel being older than you. The first plant I ever bought, back in 1967, is also older than you, and we still have it in the house. I have lots of things older than you; my books, my pots and pans, that plant, the towels. I guess that's why I felt you'd live forever, Yum Yum.

I feel strongly that there is an animal consciousness, an aura of consciousness, and that your spirit is stronger than ever, dearest Charlye. There is a uniqueness to you, to the picture you left behind, following me in every room, your eyes meeting mine wherever I turn, no matter what room I'm in.

Dearest Charlye, we love you.

Hi, dearest Charlye. It's another late night tonight. Since you're not here, we have no commitment to coming home in the evening. In some ways that's good, but in some ways it's bad. Either way, Yum Yum, we miss you terribly.

When I joke, "Isn't this a cute outfit to wear when I'm walking Charlye," Bert says sadly, "You wish."

Kathy is one of the people who works with us and she was so kind those nights I sobbed, when you were first gone. She was hurt tonight and is crying bitterly. I hope she remembers how kind she was to me when you first left us, and I was torn apart and sobbing bitterly and sadly.

I still sometimes cry bitterly and hurt terribly that you're no longer here. Yet I feel you're expanding your aura and stretching yourself. I forget that through your spiritual self you have a wider world to roam. Tonight I feel a little better, Yum Yum, and hope I can stop hurting.

In late April I found another of your bones in my paper clip box, then some in the kitchen near the toaster and a couple more in my desk at work. I love having them around, dearest Charlye. They bring me much closer to the reality of your former presence and hopefully to the aura of your existence today.

My dearest Charlye, another day, and I've just realized we've stopped counting the weeks! About ten days ago, I turned on the fan in the living room for the first time this season. How I used to worry about turning it on when you were here. I was always afraid a blade would break. Last year I said I would be brave and gamble and turn it on. I think you enjoyed it, too. When I turned it on this time, thinking of you as I did so, I rather enjoyed it, though the breeze in my face and the memory of you made it just a bit painful.

The dogs that run loose around here don't have to worry about you and me anymore. No one has to say, "Please put your dog on a leash," and on and on. A few weeks ago, the black and white dalmation was walking spiritedly with his master and mistress and I had to smile. He was loose, but I no longer have to ask them to put him on his leash. No more do I have to worry that a loose dog will come after my Charlye.

When we first came up here, we used to have little dogs and big, furious dogs coming after us. We were both afraid, but I'd scoop you into my arms and we'd protect each other. You knew I was protecting you, too! Finally, Bert made that big stick for us and we used it to fend off all those dogs until we got home. Now I use that stick, your stick, Yum Yum, to do my exercises in the morning.

I'm writing this in the "Charlye" guest room, where your picture hangs over the bed. Who would have thought how life would change and do those things to us?

It's become a terrifying reality, dearest Charlye: I'm no longer responsible for anyone but myself. The routine things we took for granted have now become a different kind of reality. There's no longer any excuse not to do anything. No "I have to walk Charlye," on a Sunday morning when I'd rather have stayed in bed. Now I can just stay in bed. The only excuse now is me, Yum Yum!

I came home from work today and realized I have no real hobbies. All I do is go to work and come home. There's nothing else I want to do. Before, I'd always said, "I have to take care of Charlye," but now there are no excuses to anything!

Good night, dear Yum Yum.

Hi, dearest Charlye. This Thursday will be almost four months. It's like a beginning and an ending…or the beginning of an ending I never believed possible. Thursday night we slept in our Charlye room. As I said my prayers and fell asleep, I thanked God for you, as I always do. I wasn't cognizant of your huge photo over my head. I'd hoped I'd dream of you, as I had when I'd felt you so strongly in my left arm two days after you died. I thought I'd wake up at night and feel your presence on the bed as I always had. I thought perhaps you'd come out of the picture. I've placed a picture of you in every room, hoping you'll come out and follow me.

You know, Yum Yum, when we lose something, we hope we'll find it, whether it be a misplaced book, a sock from the laundry, a paper with notes or anything else. Despite sleeping under your photo, though, nothing happened. I slept through the night, I didn't dream of you, and you didn't come back, Yum Yum. I come up the hill, after leaving the glass door open, but you're not there behind that door waiting for me. You aren't here in earthly presence. I put a picture in every room, yet you don't come out of any of them, Yum Yum, as we sometimes see happen in the movies.

Yum-Yum, you did die and I've got to let go. Please help me. You're not coming back and I've got to let go. Ruth Washington had three German Shepherds, but last night she told me "Cookie" will always be her favorite. She said she'll always remember Cookie's eyes looking at her as she drove her to the vet for the last time.

Your eyes look and me and follow me wherever I go; the bedroom, the kitchen, the library. I kept thinking that one picture was so special but it's still only a picture, Yum Yum. You've never walked out of it. You didn't come to me in my dreams. I didn't feel you on the bed.

Dear Charlye, you died. I have to believe it. I can't keep driving up the hill thinking maybe, just maybe you've been away but now you'll be back, waiting for me. I can't keep thinking you'll be walking around the edge of the pool if I go outside. Charlye, I'm tormented and I've got to stop! It seems I only stop thinking when I'm working. When I'm home, I see you everywhere I look. Is it that I didn't have enough time to prepare for your death? For years, Dr. Jones had said you'd live "a few more years." He gave you a clean bill of health on December 29th-February 4th you were dead! Does my internal computer need more time to process and accept this?

What's wrong with me, dearest Charlye? Do I want to punish myself? Why did my reality say you'd live as long as I? Yet, why was I so terribly worried about you when you were sick?

Last night, we rearranged the furniture in the library to break the spell of seeing you sitting on the couches. They had always been facing toward the kitchen so you could see us, but now we've moved them to give a different feel to the room. Everything we've ever done was done with you in mind, dearest Charlye. Everything!

We had lots of company this past year and I was thrilled you weren't alone as much as usual. You even came to work with us several times.

When we were rearranging the library furniture, we found one of your bones under the couch, further proof that you were actually here, Charlye. I can't, yet I must, accept that you're gone, Yum Yum.

We bought a new picture album yesterday and I put most of your pictures in it. Bert smiled when we were looking at through it. But dearest Charlye, I'm so angry...at you, at me! I'm sorry, but I loved you as I will have loved no other.

I hope you remember me when I get to your new home some twenty years from now. I hope I'll cry no more. I hope I can accept that you were once here, delicious and beautiful, but that now you're a spirit above us.

We heard a very sad story the other day, about a terminally ill little boy. He had been granted his last wish to see Mickey Mouse at Disney World in Orlando, Florida. While riding in his carriage, as he and his parents were strolling through the exhibits and displays, he suddenly began to jerk. His father ran outside with the carriage, screaming for someone to get oxygen. The mother picked the child up and in that split second, he died in her arms.

I think reading about that tragedy and it triggered my crying for you this weekend, by causing me to re-live your dying, in the bed with us, in Bert's arms.

We have been in such pain! We loved you, and always will, but the pain must subside, dearest Charlye, and I must let go.

I didn't write yesterday, dearest Charlye. I enjoy writing in bed, before I go to sleep, but I'm not sure Bert wants that. Rather than create a situation, I thought I'd do it this morning. When I came home last night, I choked on that old pain of coming to the door and no Charlye. I guess that's why I don't come home and can't bear to stay here.

I almost avoid looking at your pictures. I used to look at them thinking you'd walk out alive, or at least see me and that I'd feel you spiritually. Now I avoid looking at them. I've got to get over this pain, dearest Charlye.

On Sunday, Elliott told me, "The pain of death must go through its seasons." I must go through this pain for the year, because each season has its unique memories. I know this spring time aches terribly. I think Spring was one of your favorite seasons; smelling the wind, going out on the back porch, seeing me in the pool and coming to the edge of it to let me kiss you.

I know I couldn't wait until the end of that first week following your death. I was reliving each day of your last week as each new day came upon us. Then I counted the second week, then the third, then a month, and now it's been almost four months. So it goes, dearest Charlye. For this week I'm aching all over again. Dr. Hill calls it a void. I call it like a hole in the heart. Your absence hurts me every day, Yum Yum.

Sundays at home without you are usually a heavy date. I almost...not almost—really...want to run away on Fridays, lose Saturdays and Sundays, then come back on Mondays.

Until the other day, I'd been going out of my way to deliberately put lights over some of your pictures. I honestly thought maybe you'd see it and come out. I don't even dream about you. Nothing has happened in terms of your earthly self. You died, dearest Charlye, and I've got to believe and accept that fact.

I'm no longer responsible for anyone but myself. I can water flowers in the morning instead of walking you. I spend more time dressing since I don't have to walk you. Sometimes, I'd be too tired to want to go out with you at night. Why am I not as tired now? I've no excuse not to do anything anymore. I'm responsible only for myself, dearest Charlye. I can even spend a half hour writing to you.

Children were singing on Mother's Day and I thought of you, of the chicken and rice I'd made for you that last Sunday you were here. Bert didn't feel well this weekend, so I made chicken and noodles, but I burned the noodles. I burnt a few things this weekend. Good! If I'd made good chicken and rice, I'd have cried thinking of you. Love you, dear Charlye.

June 1, 1988

Dearest Charlye, I'm trying not to hurt as much. If I feel it coming, I try to turn it off. Tomorrow is the infamous Thursday and, if I think of it, it hurts terribly. George Walthall was here and he saw your picture in the guest room. It was good to hear someone mention your name. It made it seem that you really were here, Yum Yum. It's such a strange feeling to accept the reality that you were here, but now you're not.

Were you ever not here? Or were you not ever here, but are spiritually here now? It's so confusing to me, dearest Charlye, that I'm almost afraid to look at your pictures. Yet, I fear if I don't look, you're probably upset, as you sometimes were when I'd not realized you were underfoot and you'd bark softly to tell me you were there.

Love you, Yum Yum. Good night.

June 3, 1988

Hi, dearest Charlye. The Walthalls have a lovely, peaceful place on the lagoon in Gulf Shores and they've invited us for the weekend. It was like a gift from you to have this opportunity to get out of the house and away from the memories of happy weekends at home with you. If you were here, we wouldn't have gone, dearest Charlye and in that sense it seems so painful that I choke with sobs and tears. Nancy Walthall stopped by the house before we left, and it felt good to show her the "Charlye's" album I had put together. You came alive to me for those few moments. I really can't bear your death, dear Charlye. If I'm at work, I have a certain sense of peace, but then it's too much work-and no other activities. It's all-consuming.

There is a sense of peace in looking over the water here. The breeze is delicious. The water has a certain air of calmness and seems to evoke stillness and yet, at the same time, movement. The swimming pool at home is pretty, but it doesn't give this sense of calmness. Bounded by a fence, it doesn't give the sense of infinity that this place does.

Could we live here permanently? Could I live here alone? It's natural and calm...almost Quaker...in its simplicity. There's the soft grey color of the paint, the wooden dock, the banister, the movement of lights and cars across the waterway. A sense of peace comes over the environment.

For the first time ever, there are no man-made, electronic sounds; no television, no radio. There's only the wind, maybe passing cars and, oh yes, the whirring of the air conditioning and a boat pulling up to the dock next door. It's charming and free here, dearest Charlye, and you would have loved it. You'd have held your head high and smelled the wind. The air at home is so sticky, humid and warm, we don't smell the wind anymore. It's lovely here, Charlye, a corner of the world tucked away.

In another ten years, this will be built up terribly and I wonder if it would pay to get into the market now and build. I wonder if we'd be happy here? Would we come here every weekend? Would I get lonely? It's about 3-1/2 hours from home. Smelling the wind still reminds me of you. There is calmness in sitting here, smelling the wind, with no TV or music, only the humming of the darkness, lights, water, peace, and the infinite expanse to look beyond, with no fences to block the mind or view.

It's been a long time since I've thought about your " smelling the wind." I left the house, too, without looking at your picture or touching your urn. Sometimes, when I come home, I want to grasp that urn with power and strength. I want to wake you up. I feel almost guilty, but I'm glad I walked out of the house without turning back. I must stop thinking, Charlye, and I hope you'll understand.

I guess the memories have all been written, dearest Charlye. You're with me every day, next to my heart in my locket. You're still with me when I come home. I want to share new experiences, like tonight, with you but I can't. I can only remember you had some of this on the beach with us.

Sometimes my bed is rumpled and my first thought is, "How did Charlye get on it?" Then I remember I sat down on it to put my stockings on.

I still think about you when I make chicken soup and rice. I think about you in many ways, doing many things, particularly now, in the midst of your favorite season, with the freshness of Spring and the warmth of the sun.

I have a book in which I've kept a continuous record of your weight since 1985. I'll always have so much from you, dearest Charlye. I didn't realize how quickly our time could pass, until it had ended. I'm sorry, dearest Charlye.

A dog is barking in the distance and it sounds like echoes over the water.

Good night, dearest Charlye.

A postscript, dear Charlye. I can't seem to let go. I sob while talking to someone about a new home. I think of you walking through it, smelling the new wood, and on the beach "smelling the wind and surf," and running in the sand. You used to run with us in the sand in Virginia Beach, dear Charlye. You smelled, and you romped, and you loved it.

Now, here we are at the Gulf Shores, where we never would have come if you'd been alive, because we'd never leave you home just to go on a vacation. We had a visit with a lovely lady. She had two dogs in her car, so I struck up a conversation with her and started telling her about you. She said she'd once lost a dog through a divorce proceeding and that it had hurt her bitterly.

There's another lady who lives almost next door to this house, who presently has two dogs. One strayed into her yard the other night, and she thinks he's sick.Yum Yum, I start talking to people all because of you...in life and in death.

You're still the focal point of our lives. You're still "Our Charlye." We still see you in the sunshine and we shall see you in the night. We shall see you all of our lives, in spirit, in hope, in life, in death, and in the energies of your being, always moving towards us.

Dearest Charlye, as a post script to all my thoughts, you've unleashed my emotions: your death allowed me the respectability of crying. I didn't have to apologize for my anguish or tears. My Charlye had died and I could cry, acceptable or not, as it was to many. I couldn't stop the tears or the ache and pain of the hole in my heart. It's only been about four days since I've controlled the tears, dearest Charlye, and when I feel the ache in my heart, I cut it off. I know you understand.

I can look at your picture and feel your eyes upon me. When pain hits me from external forces, I call upon you and feel a sense of peace.

Dearest Charlye, though I can't touch you, I feel your presence watching over me, caring for me, easing my tensions, giving me the strength to do, to create, to move on and back off when necessary. I feel you speak to me when I most need it. I feel you understand the pain of my emotions, dearest Charlye! I look at you and I feel...I'm not afraid anymore.

If your earthly body could really leave me, dearest Charlye, there is nothing for me to fear, ever again. I've begun to play the musical tapes again, without crying. I love playing the tape of your barking. Oh, how I love that one. It makes me smile and laugh and feel you're here.

In the midst of this strengthening and awakening, dearest Charyle, I experienced a surge of energy about 1:00 P.M. on June 15th. I was beginning to reorganize the library and on the bottom of one of the shelves, stuck in between some papers on South Africa, there was one of your bones. It was about 7/8ths eaten and chewed, and had some of your hairs on it and some blood from your gums. I smiled with joy, dearest Charlye, and felt the happiness of your gift. In my excitement, I kissed the bone.

The total gift, what a blessing, dearest Charlye. How did you ever put it there? Were you saving it for me as a gift, as you did that picture I took of you just four days before Christmas and, unknown to me then, about six weeks before you were to die?

Dearest Charlye, thank you for you. As someone just wrote us, "in grief you have come to me and I have been productive."

I have learned from you, both before and since, and your death has allowed me to cope, to understand, to realize tomorrow we'll meet and start again! Though I don't write now, you're in my thoughts every day and I wear your photograph in the locket, resting on my heart. Ever so often, as I do my exercises, it bounces and I wonder if you feel the momentum.

I love you, dearest Charlye. I now water the plants in the morning, instead of walking you. As I look at the birds flying overhead, I wonder if they've visited with you. I should smile for your peace, but I shall always miss running to you, touching you, loving you. You are and always will be my Charlye, Carol's Charlye, and my CB handle is still "Charlye's Momma!"

Today I saw a 1988 penny in my purse. A momentous year in its beginning...thank you...for an infinite friendship that will stretch beyond time, age, and sickness, into peace, joy and strength.

Thank you, dear God, for all the growth and learning and strengthening and living. Thank you, dear God, and thank you, dearest Charlye.

Amen.

I want to write on...and write on...and hope someday over again! New searchings...new smells...new learning...

An Epilogue

Dearest Charlye:

A post script to all this writing. My emotions have been unleashed. I now know you're not here for me to run home to, to touch, to hug.

As I come up the hill at night or in the sunny daytime, an instant hurt like a panic tears me apart, but I hasten to push away the pain. I don't look at you as strongly in your pictures. Just this week, I started watching your eyes following me. I hope you're not hurt, dearest Charlye. I've had to learn to let go in order to survive without torment and agony. It comes back, particularly when we're home on Saturdays and Sundays, but I'm trying to relearn my emotions, Charlye.

I allowed myself the joy of playing some of my musical tapes last week without feeling emotionally hurt.

You're in my prayers every morning and every night. I wear the golden locket with your hair and picture inside all the time, except when I'm swimming or bathing.

Tonight we saw another import bed and said, "That would have been great for Charlye."

There's a new house in the neighborhood, built since you died, and I choked up when I passed it. I hadn't walked that way since you died. It hurt terribly that you weren't here to see this new house or smell the wood or sniff its airs.

I don't like going to the Cracker Barrel Restaurant anymore, because we used to take you with us. We'd always request a window seat so we could see you in the car and smile as we watched you looking around or resting in the front seat.

Dearest Charlye, you will be missed every day of our lives! We will sit on chairs you sat on, eat food and leave just a bit on our plates, or have crumbs falling on the floor, and we'll always smile and hurt and think, "It's Charlye's."

As we venture into new paths, walk on new roads, live in new houses, or make speeches to new audiences, your spirit will go with us. Maybe that's an enrichment. I'm less lonely now, my voids don't seem to exist.

Much of this was written in the dark during a power failure at work. I sat there writing in the dark, yet not in darkness. I felt I could write you in peace and your light and spirit would envelop me, and they have. The lights came back on some thirty minutes after I started writing to you, just as I felt they would.

Your spirit will always be with us, sharing, giving, caring, watching. Dearest Charlye, you are "My Charlye!" Bert's greatest gift to me was to give me "My Charlye!" Thank you, dearest Bert and dearest Charlye! And dearest God for making it so!

PostScript...

As of October 9, 2002, Bert and Charlye are together, and Bert's dog in Amsterdam, The Netherlands, Tommy, is romping with them.

And God said,"...when there are two or more of you, I am in the midst of you..."

Thank you, dearest God, for our blessings, for having led Bert and me to each other, and to Charlye. We chose each other, and YOU have chosen us, then, now and forever.

You continue to refresh and restore our lives, eternally and spiritually, and YOU are my hope, my trust, my source of who I am. I thank you for bringing me HOME THROUGH YOUR SPIRIT!

Charlye and Bert talking

Charlye chewing rawhide stick

Charlye in coat

Picture memorial